THEOLOGY AND SCIENTIFIC CULTURE

THOMAS F. TORRANCE

General Editor

———

VOLUME IV

AXIOMATICS AND DOGMATICS

This book is dedicated to Jan

AXIOMATICS AND DOGMATICS

JOHN R. CARNES

New York
Oxford University Press
1982

First Edition 1982 by Christian Journals Limited, BELFAST and 760 Somerset Street W, Ottawa, Ont. Canada.

Library of Congress Cataloging in Publication Data

Carnes, John Robb, 1924–
    Axiomatics and dogmatics. — (Theology and scientific culture; 4)
    Bibliography: p.
    Includes indexes
    1. Theology — Methodology 2. Axioms 3. Knowledge, Theory of (Religion) 4. Christianity and language 5. Theology, Doctrinal.
    I. Title II. Series
    BR118.C23 1982   230 82-12537

ISBN 0–19–520377–1

ISBN 0–19–520377–1

Phototypeset by Mayne, Boyd & Son, Ltd., Belfast

Cover designed by Sandy Ferguson

Made in Ireland

General Foreword

The appearance of a series of books on *Theology and Scientific Culture* indicates that we are moving beyond the old antithesis between theology and science, and that the disastrous split in our western culture between the natural and the human sciences is in process of being healed. The increasing pervasiveness of science in our modern life is due not merely to the impact of new technologies on our everyday existence, but to the fact that science has been throwing up integrative modes of thought which have far-reaching implications for knowledge in every sphere of human enterprise. To a unifying outlook of this kind theology has much to offer, as in dialogue with natural science it gains a deeper understanding of the creation through which God makes himself known to mankind. Moreover, it is more and more being realised by natural science through dialogue with theology that empirico-theoretical science as we have developed it owes not a little to the injection of Judaeo-Christian ideas about the universe and its contingent order into the framework of its regulative beliefs.

The day is fast receding when people regarded theology and science as mutually exclusive or when the natural sciences were despised by the humanities as having little to do with the finer and more intangible levels of human life and thought. All sciences, human, natural and theological, share the same concern for the integrity, authenticity and beauty of the universe in which God has placed us, the same passion for objectivity and truth in our multivariable relations with reality, and the same call for humility born of the conviction that the created order manifests a range of intelligibility that we may apprehend only as its comparatively elementary levels. Yet the more deeply we probe into the secrets of the universe, the more we become locked into a dimension of intelligibility that transcends its manifestations in the phenomenal patterns of nature and makes them point indefinitely beyond themselves. As our scientific inquiries press hard upon the boundaries of created reality, we find ourselves grasped by a commanding rationality calling for universal respect and commitment beyond the limits of our scientific experience and formalisable knowledge. As the universe unfolds the simplicity, harmony and subtlety of its order to our questioning, the more it is heard to cry out for its Creator. Thus theological and scientific inquiry have begun to overlap and bear upon each other at decisive points. We have entered upon a new age in which we are compelled to reject the old dualisms, change our received notions, and develop richer, unifying forms of thought, more adequate to an enlarged apprehension of the nature of the universe and its transcendent Creator.

The theologians and scientists who contribute to this series are all very different in training and outlook and in religious persuasion. But they all share the same concern to bridge the gap between theology and science and to find ways of developing dialogue between them on a constructive basis. There are no overall directives. Each contributor has been invited to take his own way, so that none is committed to the views of another through sharing in the same enterprise. It is to be hoped that in this way an open and fruitful dialogue will emerge in which many others beyond the immediate contributors to this series will take part.

Dr John R. Carnes makes his distinctive contribution to our series on *Theology and Scientific Culture*, not as a theologian but as a formal mathematician, and thus from the scientific role of the theology/science relationship. Although he gained his PhD in philosophy and now holds a chair of philosophy at the University of Colorado, his first two degrees were in mathematics and he was earlier employed as a physicist. More and more, however, he came to be concerned with theology, not in the field of the philosophy of religion which he considers a questionable enterprise, but in the field of the philosophy of theology where he believes all intellectually interesting problems having to do with religion are to be found. In this book which represents a merging of his main interests, mathematics and science, philosophy, and theology, he offers a critical and constructive account of theological methodology by which scientists as well as theologians will find themselves challenged.

Thomas F. Torrance

Contents

Introduction

Despite its title, this book will discuss a great many more things than axiomatic theory and dogmatic theology. Still, at the center of the discussion is my persuasion that dogmatic theology is, methodologically, essentially isomorphic with mathematics and that, as a consequence, axiomatic theory, which is the theory of pure or formal mathematics, applies also to dogmatics. If this is so, we are entitled to take Karl Barth quite seriously when he says (e.g., in the *Dogmatics in Outline*, 1949) that dogmatics is a *science*. Barth does not mean that dogmatic theology is *like* a science, or that it shares some of the characteristics of a science; dogmatics *is* a science.

This argument was advanced a few years ago in an article of mine entitled "Metamathematics and Dogmatic Theology" (1976), published in *The Scottish Journal of Theology*, and certain portions of this book can be regarded as an expansion of that article. The reason I am interested in pursuing this matter is that there is a widely held belief that theology and science are very different kinds of enterprise, so different, in fact, that some people think them to be mutually exclusive: that a scientist cannot, without sacrificing his or her intellectual integrity, take theology seriously, or vice versa. If the argument of this book is successful, I can claim to have shown this belief to be false. This will imply that the theologian and the scientist share the same concern for objectivity – for the "facts" – in their respective disciplines. More than that, however, I can claim to have shown that the results of scientific and theological inquiry are arrived at by an application of the same method. It is important that I point out at once that I am *not* proposing to examine the relationship between science and *religion*. As I will argue in the last chapters, the question of the relation between science and religion, to which so much attention has been given, rests on a mistake and cannot, therefore, be fruitfully studied. In fact, the once-fashionable "science *versus* religion" thesis has been, for the most part, abandoned, although there are still those who think we need to worry about whether such questions as the origin of the species are to be settled by an appeal to Bible or biology. To those who hold such a view, the following pages will not be very interesting.

So it is crucial, throughout a perusal of this book, to keep in mind that the discussion has to do with science and *theology*, not with science and *religion*. While, as already indicated, it is my interest in dogmatic theology and with its counterpart in pure, formal science (e.g., mathematics), that stimulated the thesis of this book and gave it its title, my argument will have to be concerned with something more than formal systems. This means that I will also think about the empirical or factual dimension of science, and that I will have to consider the empirical side of theology, which is to say, apologetics. Axiomatic theory suffices to account for the formal side of science and theology, but not for the empirical side. Therefore it will be necessary to enlarge the scope of my 1976 paper to accommodate the factual aspects of both science and theology.

In Chapter I, I will look at the relation between theories about the world and the world that those theories are about. Underlying this discussion is the premise that it is the essential function of theories to assist us in our understanding of the world, not to substitute a sophisticated and "superior" scientific view for a naive and "inferior" view. An initial effort will be made to outline the structure of scientific theories, a structure that will receive much more detailed attention in a later chapter. Chapter I will also focus on one of the difficulties with the process by which we account for the world, namely, the fact that the theories by which we seek to give such an account determine to a certain degree what the world is, i.e., that our perception of the world is "theory-laden". This calls into question our usual convictions about the objectivity of science, and an effort will be made to deal with the implied problem of subjectivism and relativism.

The structure of a scientific theory and the nature of scientific theorizing are not by any means self-evident and, in fact, are matters of some considerable dispute. Philosophers and historians of science, that is, hold different theories about the nature of scientific theories; these are called "metatheories". In Chapter II, a particular metatheory is adopted and explained. It is the function of this, and any, metatheory to provide criteria by which to tell when a cognitive structure qualifies as a theory, and what makes a theory a *good* theory. These criteria, formal, factual, and pragmatic, are discussed, with special attention given to the criterion of *explanation*: what it is for a theory to explain something.

Chapter III is parallel to Chapter I in that it attempts to show that the function of theology is to account for those kinds of experience that we call "religious" in the same way that scientific theory is designed to explain our ordinary experience of the world. Some care is taken to distinguish between religious experience, religion, theology, and philosophy: conflation of two or more of these can lead us into hopeless confusion. I argue that just as our perception of the world and its constituent "facts" is theory-laden, so our judgements about religion and the religious are "theology-laden", and that we must take care that our talk about the "facts" of religion or the data of theology does not commit us to a belief in the existence of some peculiarly "religious" phenomena that are independent of our theologies.

The acceptability of my general thesis – the isomorphism between science and theology – depends, of course, on the nature of theology: what it is, how it works, what its data are. In Chapter IV, I point out a peculiarity of the rules of the theological game, and I call this the "dogmatic inversion" or the "dogmatic turn". Essentially this means that, contrary to the conventional wisdom about these matters, dogmatics does not arrive at a concept like the fatherhood of God anthropomorphically. It is not the concept of human fatherhood that generates the idea of God the Father, but rather the other way around: we learn what it is to be a human father by first knowing the fatherhood of God. This has important implications for the data and method of theology.

Chapter V addresses the central issue of the book: that the same metatheoretical criteria apply both to scientific theory and to theology. It is not that there is one theory about theology (a metatheology) and a different theory about science; rather, there is a single metatheory that applies to both science and theology. This being the case, we are warranted in holding that science and theology are not two different kinds of intellectual enterprises, but that they are essentially the same (more properly, isomorphic), differing only in their subject matters.

After all this, the reader who is interested in substantive theological issues may well wonder what this has to do with those things that we confess in our faith. In response to this quite legitimate question, I will look (in Chapter VI) at three articles of the Creed to see how, on the basis of what has gone before, we might understand the intellectual activity that underlies the assertion of those creedal statements. It will not be my intent to provide a warrant or justification (or "proof") of those creedal assertions. Instead I will look at each from the standpoint of dogmatics and then again from the point of view of apologetics in order to see what intellectual processes are at work when one seriously and thoughtfully utters the words: "Maker of Heaven and Earth", "born of a Virgin", and "ascended into Heaven". I choose those three deliberately, because among all the propositions asserted dogmatically by Christians, those three are perhaps most offensive to the scientific temper. If my thesis can hold up under the offensiveness of those three assertions, it should be fairly solid.

In a way, with the exhibit of these three creedal formulas, my task is finished. But the discussion would seem incomplete without a consideration of the general issue of the meaning and truth of religious propositions. So I add a concluding chapter dealing with these questions. This chapter is theoretical (rather than metatheoretical), but is philosophical (rather than theological). It is at this point that my views may come into sharp contrast with those of other philosophers and philosophical theologians. For this reason, even though my discussion of meaning and truth is tangential to the central thesis of the book, it may be of more interest to some readers than other things I do in the earlier portions of the essay.

Throughout the book, I avoid partisanship with respect to substantive theological styles, positions, and issues. I do not take sides (indeed, I do not even consider) such disputes as may arise between Cullmann and Pannenberg, between theology of hope and process theology, etc. The reason is that I want to be free to accept whatever any theologian does without reference to the "rightness" or "wrongness" of his or her views, and without making judgements about the "legitimacy" or "illegitimacy" of his or her style and method. I am quite happy to accept whatever any serious-minded, intellectually responsible thinker does that he or she regards as theology, indeed as *Christian* theology.

A corollary of this is that I will not offer an *apologia* for Christianity, for Christian theology in general, or for any "school" of Christian theology. Underlying the entire essay is an acceptance of what the generous reader may be disposed to call a Christian point of view, but I do not intend to defend that point of view or my acceptance of it.

A word about scholarship. This book is not designed as a "scholarly" work in the strict sense of the term. The audience is presumed to consist of people who are intelligent and generally literate. It is not presumed to be made up of people who know the technical literature of either theology or philosophy of science, or who are particularly interested in becoming acquainted with that literature. Therefore I avoid casual references to positions or views identified by name only (e.g., "He takes a Kantian view . . .", "As in Tillich's theory . . .", "Harnack clearly showed that . . ."). If Harnack is important enough to be mentioned at all, I will give a reference and a brief explication of the relevant portion of Harnack's views. Otherwise, I will leave Harnack out of it.

I should warn my philosophically inclined readers, however, that I will be painting the philosophical and metatheoretical picture with a very wide brush. Many important questions will be begged, many important distinctions will be blurred. I do this in order to get the canvas covered; any attempt to be completely or even adequately precise in any part of the picture would bring the whole enterprise to a complete halt.

In this connection, it will be evident that I have adopted the traditional British model of scholarship over the German model, despite the fact that Americans have for many years leaned toward the latter, as evidenced by the character of their doctoral dissertations. In the German model, it is essential that one not only should know everything that has ever been written on the topic, but that one should display that knowledge by means of footnotes, bibliographical references, etc. In the British style, leading works are identified as those against which the writer's own views are to be tested. This has always seemed to me to produce a crisper and more readable work, and I hope that by adopting that model I can avoid some of the ponderousness that so often puts off the non-professional in areas like theology and philosophy.

A sabbatical leave from the University of Colorado at Boulder and a grant from the Council on Research and Creative Work of the Graduate School of the University provided the time and the resources needed for my work. It also happened that my wife was about to embark on an internship in clinical psychology at the University of Manitoba, so that we both found ourselves at Winnipeg. The libraries of the University of Winnipeg and the University of Manitoba were generous in making their materials available to me. The quiet hospitality of Canada afforded an ideal setting, at the confluence of the Assiniboine and Red Rivers, for thinking and writing.

Mention must be made of two young ladies, Calla and Helen,

who worked so hard themselves during the year in Winnipeg and who, by virtue of their own commitment to scholarship, helped materially in the completion of this project. Most of all, I am indebted to their mother, my wife, Janice. To attempt to credit, throughout the following pages, each and every one of her insightful ideas, suggestions, comments, and examples would be an impossible task. In lieu of this, I hope that she will accept my gratitude for those contributions: they are so numerous as to make this book truly a joint effort.

JOHN R. CARNES
Boulder, Colorado,
Fall, 1981.

CHAPTER I

World and Theory

One of the most important features of the development and the analysis of
modern physics is the experience that the concepts of natural language,
vaguely defined as they are, seem to be more stable in the expansion of
knowledge than the precise terms of scientific language . . . This is in fact
not surprising since the concepts of natural language are formed by the
immediate connection with reality; they represent reality . . . On the other
hand, the scientific concepts are idealizations; they are derived from
experience obtained by refined experimental tools, and are precisely
defined through axioms and definitions . . . But through the process of
idealization and precise definition, the immediate contact with reality is
lost. (Heisenberg, 1958, p. 200)

It is sometimes supposed that there are two worlds: the real world
given us in and by the sciences, and an illusory world of common
sense and ordinary experience. The real table upon which I write is
composed of atoms, which are in turn made up of nuclei and
orbiting electrons, separating which are vast amounts of empty
space. The apparently solid, continuous, impermeable table upon
which I, in my naiveté, suppose that I write is an illusion; the real
table is mostly empty space.

I begin this essay with the words of Werner Heisenberg to
emphasize an underlying premise, namely, that the above supposi-
tion is false. There are not two worlds, there is just one. It is the
function of my ordinary, sensuous, empirical experience to
acquaint me with that world. It is the function of science to explain
the world. But science obviously cannot explain the world by
substituting for it a different world. There is no such thing as the
"world of science" set over against the world of our ordinary
experience.

Science consists of theories about the world and our experience of it. Theology consists of theories about religion and the objects of religious experience. It might as well be said now, in anticipation of what is to come later, that theology is no more empowered to legislate for religion than science is to create worlds in competition with that of ordinary experience. What is given to science to be explained are such things as tables and stars, clams and begonias, feelings of love and anxiety. Similarly, it is theology's task to render an accounting of our sense of awe and wonder, of love and humility, of purposiveness and meaning, of our oneness with the world and with God. Theology is not commissioned to replace these common sense religious ideas and experiences with a set of theoretical constructs. A great deal more will be said specifically about theory in religion, i.e., theology, in later chapters.

For the time being, we will concentrate attention on scientific theory in an effort to say how theory relates to the given world and what it means for a theory to explain the world. Before doing that, however, it is necessary to say what a scientific theory *is*. This is part of the task of philosophy of science, and it must be noted that there is considerable disagreement about this matter. (For an illuminating discussion of this disagreement and recent attempts to resolve it, see Suppe, 1977.) It is not my obligation to try to settle questions about the nature of scientific theories; rather, I need only to find an acceptable account of scientific theory such that its essential elements will be adequately represented and explicated. I propose, therefore, simply to adopt a particular theory about scientific theories (a "metatheory", as it is called) without really attempting to present arguments on its behalf.

A. THE RECEIVED VIEW: A MODEL METATHEORY

The metatheory I will adopt is one that has been called (by Suppe, following Putnam, 1962) the "Received View". The reason for the name is that it is a metatheory that has, for a half century or so, been so widely accepted as to constitute a kind of orthodoxy in philosophy of science. It is, indeed, only in the past ten years or so that the Received View has come under serious and widespread attack, and even now it dominates a great deal of thinking about science, both among scientists themselves as well as among philosophers.

In its barest outlines, the Received View contends that a scientific theory:

1. is formulated in terms of an axiomatized, logical structure;
2. consists of a language that embodies
   (a) logical terms,
   (b) observational terms standing for observed or observable phenomena,
   (c) theoretical terms peculiar to the theory under consideration;
3. provides correspondence rules connecting the theoretical vocabulary with the observational vocabulary.

This is a vastly simplified form of what Suppe calls the "final version" of the Received View (1977, p. 50).

This schematism says, first, that a scientific theory is a *deductive* theory, i.e., that it is *axiomatized*. More will be said about axiomatization in Chapter II; for the moment, we need only note that the Received View maintains that a scientific theory must be (or be reducible to) a set of statements called axioms or postulates, that the working out of the theory proceeds logically from those axioms to a set of conclusions or theorems, and that everything that is not an axiom or a theorem (i.e., a statement deducible from the axioms) is excluded from the theory.

Second, the Received View says that in addition to the logical terms incorporated into the language of the theory ("not", "and", "if . . . then . . ."), there are technical terms peculiar to the theory under consideration ("mass", "gross national product", "black hole", "superego"). These terms do not necessarily refer to things that appear in our experience, but may (and typically do) refer to hypothetical entities or constructs. However, the language of the theory also contains observational terms referring to things that *do* appear in our experience ("red", "thermometer reading of 42°", "aggressive behavior", "tracks of shape S in a bubble chamber"). And, finally, connecting these two parts of the vocabulary are correspondence rules: rules that tell us how to translate theory terms (such as "neutrino") into observational language ("tracks of shape S in a bubble chamber").

The correspondence rules, then, provide a kind of bridge between the purely formal, deductive theory, and that portion of the world to which the theory is intended to apply. In the technical language of axiomatic theory, the observational vocabulary gives us, via the correspondence rules, an *interpretation* of the theoretical vocabulary. The interpretation, therefore, (1) provides a *content* for the postulates of the theory so that the theory has a factual meaning, and (2) makes possible the empirical *verification* of the theory by specifying the observables to which the scientist shall look in order to determine whether the conclusions or predictions of the theory correspond to actual states of affairs out there in the real world.

If this account of scientific theory is accepted, it would seem that a theory does what we said a theory is supposed to do, namely, to explain the world (or some portion of it). On the Received View, the data, the observed facts of the world, are fitted into the conceptual structure of the theory, thus making it possible to *think* about the world, to *understand* it in conceptual terms, rather than merely to perceive or confront it. On this view, the world has been rendered intellectually accessible.

B.   LOGICAL POSITIVISM AND THE RECEIVED VIEW

But there are problems with the Received View that we cannot ignore. The first problem is a species of "guilt by association". The Received View had its origin as part of that philosophical theory known as logical positivism or logical empiricism. To put it mildly, logical positivism is not in good repute nowadays, for reasons that will shortly become clear. Now, it might be charged that if we accept the Received View as a theory about scientific theories (and about theology), then we are also committed to adopt logical positivism as a general philosophical position. I will argue that this is not so. But first, what would be so bad about logical positivism as a philosophical framework within which to operate? What is it about this philosophy that has caused it to be so thoroughly discredited?

The essence of logical positivism is found in its theory of meaning: *a proposition is meaningful if and only if it is empirically verifiable* (or falsifiable, according to a later emendation). This "verifiability theory of meaning" was designed to rid philosophy of a class of peculiarly intractable problems in such areas as ethics, aesthetics, metaphysics, and religion. The reason we have made so little progress in those areas, positivism held, is that propositions in those areas are really pseudo-propositions. They have the grammatical form of real propositions, but are radically different in that we can specify no means for finding out whether they are true or false.

Propositions in ethics (e.g., it is wrong to cause pain unnecessarily), metaphysics (there are non-mental substances in the world), or religion (God loves us) appear to be significant assertions (like, ticks have eight legs), but in fact are literal non-sense (like, anxiety is the square root of magenta). And they are non-sense, according to the verifiability theory, because there is *in principle* no way of empirically verifying them.

This very strong meaning criterion seemed, to many philosophers, to throw out the baby with the bath water. Is it really possible to believe that for all these centuries, we have all been blethering non-sense when we talked about justice and beauty and reality, and about God? In fact, as critics lost no time in observing, logical positivism itself would appear to be on shaky ground. For consider: is the verifiability theory of meaning (italicized in the preceeding paragraph) empirically verifiable? Obviously not. Then it is equally non-sense. Logical positivism has condemned itself by its own theory of meaning.

In response to this intolerable situation, positivism modified its meaning criterion by inserting the word "cognitively" into it: A proposition is *cognitively* meaningful if and only if . . . A proposition such as "God is love" may, then, be meaningful, but its meaning is not cognitive – it does not convey any information about anything, but only expresses a feeling, or something like that. This maneuver spawned a whole series of "non-cognitive" theories in ethics, religion, and even law. As a result, many of the things that had been swept out philosophy's front door with the broom of verifiability came trooping in the back door under the banner of non-cognitivism. (In the concluding chapter of this book, we will have occasion to consider briefly one of these non-cognitive theories about religion.)

But this, of course, deprived positivism of a great deal of its force. The original idea was to rid us of these troublesome questions in ethics, metaphysics, and religion. But if it makes sense to say such things as "God loves us", even though that sense is "non-cognitive", it would appear that positivism has, at most, denied to such utterances the honorific title "cognitive".

The Received View came into being as logical positivism's philosophy of science. A moment's reflection on the characteristics of the Received View as displayed above will suffice to bring out the consonance between the general philosophical position and its philosophy of science. Our question now is whether we are committed to accept the whole of logical positivism with all its difficulties if we adopt the Received View as our metatheory. The answer is no, and the reason for that answer is that the scope or "domain" of the Received View is much more restricted than, and is strictly speaking independent of, the grander sweep of logical positivism. The proponent of the Received View says, in effect, "I am prepared to tell you what a scientific theory is and how it functions; but I have nothing to say about religion or morality or art or even, indeed, about reality itself". The logical positivist, on the other hand, says "I have a theory that will tell whether any proposition you utter is meaningful, whether in science or religion or morality, and what you must do to decide whether such a proposition, if meaningful, is in fact true". The Received View says, "Whatever it is we know by means of the sciences, here is the way we know it". Logical positivism says, "Whatever we know, we know by means of the sciences". Clearly, the former does not entail the latter.

C. A DIFFICULTY IN THE RECEIVED VIEW

However, having disposed of this "guilt by association" argument against the Received View, we have to consider another and more serious problem. It will be recalled that according to the Received View, a scientific theory has a theoretical vocabulary and an observational vocabulary. Roughly speaking, the former consists of the basic terms of the theory put together into those propositions we call the axioms or postulates, while the latter, the observational vocabulary, stands for the observable entities in that part of the real world to which the theory is designed to apply. This seems straightforward enough. We cannot observe a black hole directly, because, by definition, a black hole is a celestial body whose gravitational field is so strong that not even electromagnetic radiation can escape it. Since we observe celestial bodies by means of such radiation (light or radio waves), it follows that black holes are in principle unobservable. Therefore, in order to find out anything about black holes, we must look at other celestial bodies, namely, observable stars, whose behavior is affected by the magnetic field of a black hole. "Black hole" is, accordingly, a theoretical term in astronomy, while "behavior of (observable) stars S_1, S_2, S_3" is part of the observational vocabulary.

Unfortunately, things are not as straightforward as they appear to be. How do we observe the (observable) stars? Normally, by means of radio telescopes, that is, by the detection and recording of radio signals from those stars. But then it would seem that we do not observe the stars themselves, but only the radio signals. Hence, "behavior of (observable) stars" will have to be part of the theoretical vocabulary, to be replaced in the observational vocabulary by such terms as "radio signals".

But the same argument can be repeated for radio signals; what we actually observe are not the radio signals themselves, but meters and dials and oscilloscopes. Hence, "radio signal" becomes a theoretical term, and we have a new set of observational terms standing for meter readings and oscilloscope patterns. At each stage, of course, a new set of correspondence rules must be introduced, connecting the old observational (now theoretical) terms with the newly introduced observational terms.

Is there any place where this process comes to a halt? Are there any incorrigibly observational terms? Logical positivism sought these in what were called "protocol sentences" such as "I, John, am now experiencing a sensation of red". Such sentences were thought to be incorrigibly observational, inasmuch as they constitute reports of immediate experience. But this will not do either: even such sentences as these contain irreducibly general terms (such as "red") and other terms (such as "now") that cannot be understood as simply expressing immediate experience.

Thus, on the Received View, the observational part of the theoretical/observational distinction recedes into the elusive protocol sentence and from there disappears altogether. What started out as straightforward observational language turns out, at every stage, to be really part of the theoretical language. Theory has literally gobbled up reality. If this is so, scientific theory cannot fulfill its task, which was to explain the world, for we have lost all those observational terms that stand for the concepts formed "by the immediate connection with reality", as Heisenberg put it.

If we cannot find a way around this difficulty, then we will have to abandon the Received View, as, indeed, according to Suppe (1977, pp. 62 ff.) it has been abandoned by most philosophers of science. Happily, however, there is a way around it, and Suppe himself suggests the route. (Note that there may be *other* reasons for rejecting the Received View, so that the mere fact that we can avoid the problem at hand does not constitute a validation of the Received View.)

What we are dealing with here might be called the problem of *theoretical idealism*. Once the observational vocabulary of a theory has been absorbed into the theoretical language, the real world, so far as that theory is concerned, is nothing other than that which is contained in the theory itself. Within the domain of that theory, reality is what the theory says it is.

The way around this problem goes through a distinction between an *instrumentalist* and a *realist* interpretation of the Received View (Suppe, 1977, pp. 29 ff.). Since these are interpretations *of* the Received View, there is nothing about the Received View that can tell us which interpretation to adopt. On the *instrumentalist* interpretation, it is the function of scientific theories to make predictions about the phenomena that will be observed under specified experimental or observational conditions. The only meaning attributable to scientific statements has to do with the *phenomena*; questions as to what is "really" out there giving rise to those phenomena cannot be raised in the context of scientific theories, nor are such questions of any scientific interest.

On this interpretation, the physicist makes no commitment to a belief in the existence of anything out there called a neutrino, nor does the psychologist commit himself to a belief that there exists a thing in here called a superego. All the physicist says is that if his theory is "true", we will observe tracks of a certain shape in a bubble chamber under specified conditions. Whether those tracks are "caused" by a "thing" called a "neutrino" is of no interest to him; indeed, the question is devoid of scientific meaning. The superego is a theoretical construct, the purpose of which is to enable the psychologist to conceptualize psychological processes, the better to deal with their malfunctions. The superego is not to be understood as a little spook inside me.

D. REALISM

A *realist* interpretation of the Received View, on the other hand, holds that scientific theory carries with it a commitment to a belief in the reality of those things that constitute the denotation of the terms of the theoretical language of the theory. On a realist view, there really are neutrinos out there and superegos in here.

If instrumentalism carries the day, then reality has been divorced from theory, the way is open for a theoretical idealism, and there is no way to claim that science has explained the world. Again, if this is the case, then we would have to abandon the Received View as a metatheory. So the question is whether there are considerations that would justify our adoption of the realist, over the instrumentalist, interpretation. Certainly the motivation for doing so is very strong. We want to know whether there are neutrinos and black holes out there, and whether there are DNA molecules and superegos in here. To be told that it doesn't make any difference, as long as *scientists* can conduct their business satisfactorily is bound to be profoundly unsatisfying to *us*. Indeed, it is rather difficult to understand how or why there would ever have been such an enterprise as science if it were not for an antecedent curiosity about what is out there and in here.

Suppe puts this point more formally:

> to allow theoretical terms while holding an instrumentalism leaves one in the uncomfortable position of holding that theoretical terms are necessary, but they do not mean anything or refer to anything. Rather than maintain such a position, most people who accept the legitimacy of theoretical terms in scientific theorizing also commit themselves to the position that they have real referents in the world. (1977, pp. 34 f.)

Note, first, that science does not – and cannot – prove that there is a world out there to be explained. To do so, science would have, so to speak, to stand outside itself and its own theories; science would have to take a kind of supramundane point of view in order to ascertain the existence and nature of the world and the relation of its own theories to the world. But that, of course, is impossible.

In addition, however, note that the commitment to the existence of a real world is not something that is laid on the sciences from the outside; for example, by an arbitrary philosophical decree. Rather, the commitment to the reality of the referents of theoretical terms comes out of the nature of scientific theories themselves. The argument for realism, therefore, is not based on some prior philosophy, but arises out of an examination of the actual process of scientific theorizing. Such an examination, Suppe contends, is pushing philosophy of science in the direction of "a hard-nosed metaphysical and epistemological realism" (1977, p. 618).

Given this realist interpretation of the Received View, it is *possible* for observational terms to stand for things out there, and, accordingly, it is possible for scientific theory to explain the real world, simply because we have committed ourselves to the position that there is a real world out there for scientific theory to explain.

It might be noted also, almost parenthetically, that the decision between an instrumentalist and a realist interpretation of theory is one that must be made in theology as well as in science. The objection that many have had to Bultmann's existential theology, for example (1964), is that with his emphasis on the "internality" of religious experience, it seems to make little difference whether Jesus was crucified at some point in history, or whether he was in fact raised from the dead, or even perhaps whether there was such an historical person as Jesus of Nazareth. Bultmann's theology, so the objection goes, has been cut loose from any reference to the external reality of those things for which the theological terms appear to stand. This is, to most people, extremely disquieting: as in science we want to know whether there really are black holes and superegos, so in theology, we want to know whether in fact there was a man Jesus, and whether that man was in fact the Christ. In theology, as in science, there is the same pressure in the direction of a realist, and away from an instrumentalist, interpretation of theory.

We are not yet out of the woods, of course. Even if we accede to the demand for realism, we have to say *how* theory and world are related: it is not enough merely to assert the *possibility* that observational terms stand for real things. What seems to be presupposed in the Received View is that there is some sort of neutral territory on which theory and world meet. That territory has traditionally been supposed to lie in the process of *observation*. Since observation is *of* the world, it is not *part of* the world (except in the sense that any psychological phenomenon is part of the world). Since it is the process of observation and the facts that are disclosed in observation that give rise to and eventually confirm (or disconfirm) theories, observation is not a part of theory either. So observation is a bridge, as it were, between theory and world.

E.   THEORY-LADEN OBSERVATION

On this account of observation, the observer is like a camera, the function of which is merely to record what is out there. The record of such observations – the "facts" – then offers up the data for the theory. This is a very appealing model of observation, and it is most important to see that it runs into serious difficulty (see Hanson, 1969 and 1971). In particular, the problem is that neither observation nor the facts disclosed by observation are neutral; rather, they are "theory-laden" (Hanson, 1969, p. 131 and elsewhere). What is observed and what constitutes a fact depend in part on what we, the observers, bring to the process of observation. That is, the knowledge and beliefs that we hold play a *constitutive* role in determining what we observe.

As a simple example, consider the following figure:⬚. We know that what is there is a two-dimensional configuration of straight-line segments. But that is not what most of us *see*; what we see is a three-dimensional object, a cube. In Hanson's language, we see this two-dimensional figure *as* a cube. A somewhat more interesting example is afforded by the familiar Köhler goblet: ▮▮ . What I see in this figure depends on what I am *prepared* to see. I may at first see only the ornate chalice; but after someone tells me a story about two people in close conversation behind a closed blind, I then may see the drawing *as* a pair of silhouetted faces. I may be tempted to ask, but what is it *really* that I am seeing? There is, of course, no answer to that question, and the reason there is no answer, according to Hanson, is that there is no simple, neutral act of seeing. The camera model ("brute empiricism", Hanson calls it, 1971, p. 13) is just wrong. *Seeing* is *seeing-as* (1969, Ch. 6). All observing, and all "facts" observed, are infected by the prior knowledge, beliefs, suppositions, attitudes that we bring to the observing process.

As already noted, Hanson describes this state of affairs by saying that observation is "theory-laden". That, however, is too restrictive: theories are intellectual constructions, and our observation is laden with more than just the products of our intellects. My seeing the duckrabbit: ⌒ *as* a duck or *as* a rabbit is not the result of my having any ornithological or mammalian theories, although it does at least require that I know what a duck or what a rabbit looks like.

I am suggesting that what we observe depends on a range of beliefs that includes far more than just our theories. For example, we may distinguish a number of different kinds of snow, depending on our interests – scientific, athletic, or aesthetic. And we may suppose that the Eskimo makes many finer distinctions, because snow is so essential to the Eskimo's survival. And so he does, but not quite for that reason. According to the anthropologist, Edmund

Carpenter, the Eskimo

use many words for snow which permit fine distinctions, not simply because they are much concerned with snow, but because snow takes its form from the actions in which it participates: sledding, falling, igloo-building. Different kinds of snow are brought into existence by the Eskimo as they experience their environment and speak; words do not label things already there. Words are like the knife of the carver. They free the idea, the thing, from the general formlessness of the outside. As man speaks, not only is his language in a state of birth, but also the very thing about which he is talking. (1973, p. 43)

As Hanson says, we all have "spectacles behind our eyes" (1969, Ch. 9). The way the world looks to me depends on the particular kind of spectacles I have. Clearly, the Eskimo's spectacles reveal to him a world that looks quite different from my world. It cannot be said that the Eskimo and I see the same things, observe the same facts, and only describe them differently. The Eskimo's "facts" are not the same as my "facts". He and I do not see the same things.

Now, of course, this is not because the Eskimo has one theory about the world and I have a different theory. The Eskimo, presumably, does not have a theory about the world at all; and, for that matter, neither do I. The spectacles behind our eyes are not theoretical spectacles at all. To avoid the intellectualistic implications of the word "theory" (or of *Weltanschauung,* as philosophers are fond of saying), R. M. Hare (in Flew and MacIntyre, 1955) coined the word "blik" to stand for those non-verifiable, non-falsifiable world-perspectives or world-views which determine for us what there is out there and how it shall be known. I will adopt Hare's word because of its "neutrality" and will sometimes speak of observations and facts being blik-laden, rather than theory-laden, to keep in our minds the fact that observation is guided and shaped by factors other than our intellectual commitments.

We need to remind ourselves that the problem that led us into this discussion of Hanson's views is the problem of finding the connecting point between theory and world, and that this, in turn, is necessary in order that theory might explain the world. Hanson's view suggests that the relation between theory and world is considerably more complicated than we might have supposed at the outset. In particular, the neutral territory on which we supposed theory and world to meet, namely, observation, has been shown to be infected by our bliks and theories – the very theories that we hoped to verify by means of those neutral observations. This can be looked on as a distressing corroboration of the difficulty we encountered in the Received View by virtue of which "theory gobbles up reality". In Hanson's view, every time we try to grasp the bare facts, we find that theory has gotten there first and has already staked out its claim.

The implications of this problem for theology are apparent. If Hanson is right, then we will necessarily look at religion and religious experience through the eyes of theory – in this case, theology. We can no more take off our theological spectacles and see the "religious facts" than the Eskimo can put aside his blik and see the world as it "really" is. Thus, for example, one can no more separate the "real" Jesus (the Jesus of history) from the religiously perceived Jesus (the Christ of faith) than one can separate the "real" duckrabbit from the perceived duck. To do so would be to take off the spectacles from behind our eyes, and this is impossible.

F. THE CHALLENGE OF RELATIVISM

The success of a realist interpretation of the Received View may now appear to have been a Pyrrhic victory. There may be a real world out there for science to explain, but the nature of that real world is shaped by the very theories that we hoped to confirm or disconfirm by observation of the world. The confidence of a "hard-nosed realism" would seem to have given way to a kind of subjective relativism: the world is whatever it appears to be as seen through the particular spectacles behind someone's eyes. But, no, this goes too far. Between an objective, hard-nosed realism and a subjective relativism there is a middle route. To be sure, the world is not given to us inviolate in a set of paradigmatic observations; neither, on the other hand, are we at liberty to construct or reconstruct the world to fit our theories. Facts, Hanson says, "are what they are irrespective of anyone's pet theory to the contrary" (1971, p. 11).

It should also be said that although we may be at liberty to construct theories in any way that pleases or amuses us, theories that are built arbitrarily or in disregard of the nature of the real world are not likely to be very interesting and will surely not be useful. In fact, whatever the logic of pure-theory-building may be, we do not construct theories out of thin air, but rather with one eye on the facts that those theories are supposed to explain. More will be said about the logic of theories in the next chapter. For the moment, I only wish to point out that if, as Hanson says, observation and facts are theory-laden, the other side of the coin is that theories are "fact-laden". As theoretical structures are loaded into our observations of the world, so those observations are loaded into the theories by means of which we undertake to explain the world.

Thus, the relation between theory and world is one that we might call dialectical or recursive. The intractability of that which is given in experience sets the boundaries for theory; but new and revised theory requires that we look at the world anew. We reassess our understanding of the world on the basis of theory, and we reassess theories on the basis of our observations of the world. Using some terminology of Piaget (1971, e.g.), we might describe this dialectical relationship as one of assimilation and accommodation: we assimilate the world to our theories, and we accommodate our theories to the world.

As the reference to Piaget suggests, this dialectical relationship is not very mysterious and can itself be the object of rational, scientific study. Thus, in addition to examining the world views of the Eskimo, science can examine its own world views or bliks: its own presuppositions and methods. These concerns are the domains of inquiries such as the philosophy, the history, the sociology, and the psychology of science.

But, it may be objected, this only pushes relativity and subjectivity up one notch. Instead of confronting subjectivity in science, we now relocate it in philosophy, history, sociology, or psychology. The historian of science, for example, has its own blik, his own theories, and so his investigation of the history of some particular field of science, physics perhaps, will itself be theory- and blik-laden. If we try to escape this relativity in the history of science by moving yet another notch higher to study the philosophy of history, or the sociology of knowledge, we will encounter the same relativity at that level.

Thus, by admitting the theory-laden character of scientific observation, it would seem that we are driven to an infinite stacking of theories and metatheories, such that our efforts to deal with relativity at one level in the stack only generates the next higher level with its own relativity, and so on *ad infinitum*. It should at least be recognized that there are philosophical points of view from which to argue that the stack is *not* infinite, that in fact there is a highest level of "absolute objectivity", and that once that level is reached, the inquirer is enabled to make judgments of unchallengeable validity with respect to all lower levels of investigation. Such a philosophical theory is characteristic of Platonism; it will be recalled that Plato called that highest level the Idea of the Good.

Platonism is not popular these days; but even if one rejects the notion of an absolute standard, it does not follow that we are trapped in a paralyzing relativism according to which every theory is just as good as the next. There are ways of dealing with problems of theory at any given level that do not involve recourse to some (real or supposed) ultimate criterion of truth and validity. If – to pose an analogy – the pipes spring a leak between the lobby and the mezzanine, the plumber does not need to go to the 85th floor to solve the problem. He simply locates the leak and sets about repairing it. Our problem is a leaky theory in physics or anthropology or history – or, of course, in theology. A question has arisen about presuppositions or methods of inquiry or about the spectacles behind the inquirer's eyes. The resolution of that question will be sought in a metatheoretical inquiry: we will move up one, but only one, notch in the stack.

G.   THE DEMANDS OF OBJECTIVITY

But note, first, that it is always possible that such a question does not arise. If the pipes do not leak, we need not involve the plumber at all; if our theories are working satisfactorily, metatheoretical questions simply do not come up and there is no particular virtue in raising them arbitrarily. Sufficient unto the day are the problems thereof: we will have theoretical and metatheoretical problems aplenty without searching for them.

Note, second, however, that when questions about presuppositions *do* arise, the only reasonable demand that can be made upon us is that we be able to respond to those questions on the basis of some clearly identifiable and intelligibly formulated principles and procedures. Such principles and procedures may be available at the next highest level in the stack. If our disagreements and difficulties concerning level N in the stack can be resolved by an appeal to agreed-on metatheoretical principles at level N+1, then the matter is settled. Rationality and objectivity, that is, do not require some highest level, some Platonic absolute, in terms of which to judge all else. This is to say that objectivity has to do with the ways in which we ask and answer questions, not with some pre-ordained, final standard of truth.

To make all this a bit more concrete, suppose we go (or are pushed) to the extreme and say that in the last analysis the facts of science are ineluctably infected by theory and by our bliks, and therefore there can be no hope of a "final" objectivity in science. We might respond to this state of affairs by expressing the hope or conviction that even though we cannot find objectivity in scientific theory itself, we can insure objectivity by a metatheory (at level N+1) which specifies the criteria to be met by an acceptable scientific theory (at level N). Although the N-level theory may necessarily involve subjective elements, the (N+1)-level metatheory does not. The criteria of such a metatheory may, for example, be found among candidates such as simplicity, social utility, or acceptability to the bulk of other N-level scientists.

But suppose a critic now suggests that a metatheoretical criterion such as simplicity is itself subjective. The reason that the metatheorist takes refuge in simplicity, so the critic might say, is not that there is something rational or objectively desirable about the simplicity of scientific theories, but that the metatheorist is overly conservative or timid: in general, that the metatheory in question is infected by subjective elements arising out of the psychological make-up of the metatheorist. So, the critic might continue, what we need is a study of the psychology of metatheory before we can make judgments about the adequacy of (N+1)-level theories. What the critic calls for is an investigation at a meta-metatheoretical (N+2) level.

It is, of course, *possible* to keep going indefinitely in this fashion. But it is far from self-evident that we *must* do so. And, in fact, an examination of the history of science indicates quite clearly that we need not and do not. The plumber is able to fix the leak without re-engineering the entire system; theories are proposed, adopted, disrupted, repaired, rejected, and replaced almost continuously without disappearing into the vapors of super-metatheory.

It would, therefore, seem to be the case that our worries about subjective relativism were not so well founded as to prevent us from taking seriously the idea of scientific objectivity, even though the kind of objectivity we end up with may not be altogether satisfying to the more Platonistically inclined among us.

H. SUMMARY

Let us briefly retrace our steps in this discussion. We began with the premise that the function of theory — in science as in theology —

is to help us to understand, i.e., to explain, the world. For an account of what a theory is and how it works, we turned to the Received View. But we found that a problem in the Received View, namely, the relation between the observational and theoretical vocabularies, threatened to split theory apart from the world, thus making it impossible for theory to explain the world.

The way out of that difficulty lay through a realist interpretation of the Received View. No sooner had we found our way out of that thicket, however, than we ran into Hanson's contention that observations and facts are theory-laden, that theory itself determines, at least in part, the nature of the world that the theory is supposed to explain. So it seemed that we were back in a kind of relativism according to which the world is whatever our theories say it is.

As it turned out, however, the problem was not as bad as it seemed: the anarchy of relativism, we found, could be overcome by specifying (at the metalevel) those criteria which must be satisfied by a theory in order that the theory be adequate, such specification itself, of course, being always subject to criticisms at higher metalevels.

The effect of this is to say that there is a real world to which theory refers (the realist interpretation) and that we can specify how theory and world are related (scientific objectivity), even though that relation may not be as simple as brute empiricism (the camera model) would have led us to suppose. Against this background, we are now ready to consider the theoretical spectacles – the presuppositions of theory in both science and theology – through which we view the world, and to that task we turn our attention.

CHAPTER II

Criteriology: A Metatheoretical Discourse

In Chapter I we affirmed a relation between scientific theory and ordinary experience, between scientific language and our ordinary language and the concepts it embodies, along the lines suggested by Werner Heisenberg. This affirmation led us in the direction of what Suppe calls "a hard-nosed metaphysical and epistemological realism", which is to say that it is of the very nature of scientific theorizing to find itself committed to the position that the technical terms of scientific theory have real referents in the external world. Note that this is not a requirement laid on the sciences by a realist philosophy; rather, a philosophical realism is implicit in the very process of scientific theorizing itself.

This is reassuring. It may be of particular comfort to those who do theology to find that if the analogy between science and theology holds up, the commitment to the reality of the referents of theology is as justifiable as science's commitment to the reality of those things to which its technical vocabulary refers. But that reassurance is clouded over by considerations in which we found that our observations, and our judgements of what are the "facts" are formed and shaped by the very theory that those facts are intended to support and verify. A disturbing circularity seems to be built into our theoretical processes: a theory, it might seem, is able to explain the facts because it determines what those facts are to begin with. More generally, our notions of what the world is and what it contains is a function of an antecedent world view, a

Weltanschauung, a blik that incorporates both our theories and those more fundamental perspectives grounded in our subconscious or even neurological processes.

Thus it appears that despite our realism, we are not entitled to believe that there exists a simple correspondence between the language of theory and the referents of theory "out there" like the correspondence between a photograph and its object. Accordingly, chastened by these results, we now approach questions of "fact" more cautiously than before. However, avoiding naive realism (which says that the world *is* as it *appears to be*) does not mean that we embrace theoretical idealism (which holds that the world is whatever our theories say it is). We do not construct the world and we cannot create facts by the mere intellectual process of generating theories. Were that the case, we could discover the nature of the world simply by analyzing the internal structure of our theories. As we will shortly see, consistency is an essential feature of any theory; but nothing guarantees that a consistent theory is a true or adequate theory.

In fact, what preserves scientific objectivity in the face of the theory-laden relativism of Chapter I is what might be called a recursive or dialectical relation between theory and world. Theory is self-corrective, not in the sense of building more and more elaborate intellectual structures that will culminate in The Truth, but in the more prosaic sense that each time the theory dips into the world of fact, the theory must be corrected or amended.

But, according to Chapter I, the amendment of theory leads, or may lead, to further restructuring of the world and its constituent facts, which again produces a modification of theory. Only if theory and fact are understood in isolation from each other do we need to worry about "final" truth in theory and "ultimate" facticity in the world. We are instead dealing with the more fruitful notion that, in William James's words, truth *happens to* an idea, a theory. And, we might add, instructed by the Eskimo experience, reality happens to the world.

Philosophy has, traditionally, held two opposing ideas about the nature of truth: the correspondence theory, and the coherence theory. The latter theory was characteristic of idealist metaphysics. If the world consists of ideas and the minds that house those ideas, *and nothing else,* then there is no sense to a criterion of truth that leads us to seek for the extra-mental concomitants of our ideas. There *is* no extra-mental world in which to seek. Therefore, truth is resident in our ideas themselves, and consists in the coherence of those ideas with each other.

With the rise to dominance of empiricism, especially in England and America, metaphysical idealism gave way to some form of realism. As a result, the coherence theory of truth was supplanted by the correspondence theory, holding that the truth of an idea or of a theory lies in its correspondence with the external world of fact. Obviously, this understanding of the nature of truth fits more comfortably with the scientific temper, and each reinforced the other.

Our discussion of the preceding chapter must not lead us to lose sight of the point of the correspondence theory of truth. Scientific theory is about the world, and the realities of the world are ultimately responsible for confirming or disconfirming those theories. But as noted, the correspondence between theory and world cannot be viewed as anything so simple and obvious as the relation between a photograph and what the photograph is a photograph of.

In view of the theory-laden character of our knowledge of the world, in view of the fact that theory plays a much more constitutive role than naive empiricism would have us believe, the internal nature of theory becomes more important than might otherwise be the case. On a naively empiricist view, the internal character of theory was not so crucial, since the *observabilia* of the world out there would sooner or later tell us what we needed to know about our theories. But if those *observabilia* are themselves formed by theory, it behooves us to be more attentive to the "internal" attributes of theory, and this, in some way and measure, brings us back around to the coherence theory. Just as, therefore, we found it necessary to steer a middle course between naive realism and a theory-laden relativism, so now we are obliged to balance off a coherence with a correspondence approach to the evaluation of scientific theory.

According to the Received View, outlined in Chapter I, theory consists of two parts: a "formal" part, the axiomatic system; and the interpretation, giving the theory its factual content. The "formal" axiomatic is the logical armature or skeleton of the theory; the empirical character of the theory is given by its interpretation. Each of these two elements has its own set of criteria, and I will call them the "formal" and "empirical" criteria.

In addition to the formal and empirical criteria (which correspond loosely to the internal and external, or to the coherence and correspondence, dimensions of the evaluation of the theory), there are what I will call "pragmatic" considerations that we bring to bear on theories. These have to do with the utility of theories – for example, their aesthetic qualities. More will be said about this later.

For the time being, I want to focus our attention on the internal, the formal criteria of theories. We should not lose sight of the ultimate reason for doing this. Theologies are theories about religion and the religious experience. What passes muster as a religious experience, what constitutes the content of religion, and what, therefore, theology has to work with, depends on the theological "spectacles behind our eyes". If that is correct, then what we have to say about the formal characteristics of scientific theory will be central to our views of theology as well.

A. *Criteria*   I have mentioned the formal and empirical *criteria* of theories. But what is a criterion? How does it pertain to our discussion of theory? Where does it fit into the Received View as an analysis of theory? To say that a characteristic C is a criterion for something T is to make two separate but related assertions. (1) We mean that C is the characteristic that makes T a T; C makes T the particular kind of thing it is. (2) We mean that we tell whether T is a good T by seeing whether or to what extent the characteristic C is manifested by T. This all sounds more formidable than it really is, as it will become evident in the following example. What are the characteristics that make something an automobile? There may be differences of opinion on this, but a minimum list can probably be specified; such a list would set forth the "necessary and sufficient conditions" for calling something an automobile. Among these characteristics would be an internal combustion engine, a certain number of non-flanged wheels, a transmission connecting the engine with the wheels via an axle, a steering mechanism, etc. These are the characteristics which, if manifested by the particular piece of equipment before us, would justify our calling it an automobile. These characteristics are, then, criteria in sense (1) above.

Subsequently I will call them *constitutive* criteria. The constitutive criteria for automoticity, then, are those characteristics the presence of which is necessary and sufficient to justify our calling something an automobile.

Suppose, however, that before us is an automobile-like structure which, on inspection, turns out to have four wheels, a transmission, an engine, a steering mechanism, and so on, but whose differential is inoperative so that both rear wheels must rotate at the same rate. No doubt, we would call this an automobile, but not a very *good* one, and we would recommend that it be taken to a garage to be repaired. The characteristics in our specified list now begin to function in sense (2) above: the presence or absence, or the degree of presence or absence, of one or more of them determines whether we regard the automobile as a *good* automobile.

Note that in both senses (1) and (2), the characteristics of our agreed list function in an evaluative or "normative" way. In sense (1), the presence or absence of the characteristics indicate when I am *justified* or *warranted* in calling this thing an automobile; in sense (2), the presence or absence or the degree of presence or absence of the characteristics are appealed to in determining when the car is a *good* car. It is this normative role of the characteristics that leads me to call them *criteria*.

Senses (1) and (2) are rather closely related, as is suggested by asking how bad a car has to be (sense 2) before it ceases to be a car at all (sense 1). If the differential is inoperative and the engine is running on only three cylinders, I would say that my car is not in very good shape. But suppose the differential to be inoperative, the engine to have fallen out, the wheels stolen, the battery dead, and the steering mechanism broken. Do I still speak of this object as an automobile? At some point, the criteria for 'automoticity' would be so far from fulfillment that I would refuse to call the heap before me an automobile. At some point, that is, senses (1) and (2) "converge".

In talking about formal and empirical criteria for scientific (and, ultimately, for theological) theories, we will need to have both senses (1) and (2) in mind. We might say that an ideal theory is one that fulfills each of the several criteria in a complete and ideal way. It is highly unlikely that any theory does that, either in science or in theology. This only means, however, that theories are typically to be evaluated in terms of more-or-less, better-or-worse, adequate-or-inadequate, rather than in more definitive terms such as true-or-false.

B. *The Received View: Constitutive Criteria.* On the Received View, which is here taken as a kind of model metatheory, there are three elements that are constitutive of a scientific theory (see p. 3, above):

1. it is axiomatized;
2. its language involves:
   (a) logical terms,
   (b) observational terms,
   (c) theoretical (or technical) terms;
3. it incorporates correspondence rules relating the theoretical to the observational vocabulary.

I will discuss in some detail the matter of axiomatization in section C below, but for the time being, I need only observe that one of the *desiderata* of all theoretical activity is to pare the theoretical apparatus down to its bare minimum with regard to its fundamental vocabulary and its assumptions or postulates, and to make that apparatus approximate as closely as possible to a deductive system in which all conclusions follow from the basic assumptions or postulates with no intrusion of material from outside the domain of the theory itself. This is nothing more nor less than the spirit that drives axiomatization.

Moreover, any theory recognizes the need for a vocabulary that expresses adequately and precisely what the theory is saying: a theoretical vocabulary peculiar to that theory. But there needs to be some bridge between that language and the ordinary language in which we conceptualize the world to which the theory refers. This, in essence, is what is involved in criteria 2 (*b, c*) and 3 above.

What I am suggesting is that the Received View does not make excessive demands on theory, but that, instead, my simplified version of that view represents in outline what any theory ordinarily sets out to achieve. If axiomatization is an ideal for theories, and if a particular theory fails to achieve axiomatization, it is not necessary to go so far as to deny that such a theory is scientific at all (a move that is sometimes made with respect to the social sciences; see e.g., Rudner, 1966). It may be true that the *less* formalized a theory is, the more it suffers in comparison with a *more* formalized theory, other things being equal. But it is rarely the case that other things *are* equal. Thus one cannot hang the entire weight of the evaluation of theory on this – or on any other – single criterion.

I call (1)-(3), above, "constitutive" criteria because, on the model I have adopted, these characteristics are the most general attributes that any theory must satisfy; they specify the elements that *constitute* any theory. We now move to a set of criteria that deal with the inner workings of a theory so constituted.

C. *Formal Criteria.* A great deal of what we know about metatheory – the theory of theories – comes from that discipline known as metamathematics. The reason why metamathematics developed so early, in contrast with the theory of empirical theories (such as chemistry or biology) is obviously that mathematics itself developed quite fully at a very early date, specifically, with Euclid. Empirical theory, in the modern sense at least, did not appear on the scene until the 17th century and it was a long time until scientific processes became canonized to the point where it was profitable to metatheorize about the fledgling scientific theories. We are, however, concerned only with the formal aspect of theories at the moment.

A formal, or axiomatic, system consists of a set of undefined terms (the "primitives"), a set of unproved propositions (the axioms), and a set of rules of inference (the logic) by which we infer one proposition (a theorem) from other propositions (axioms or already-proved theorems). Actually, the primitive terms are not just undefin*ed,* but are undefin*able,* within the system under consideration. Those terms might be defined with reference to some concepts that lie outside this particular axiomatic system; but the constitutive criteria (above) stipulate that part of what we mean by an axiomatic system is that it be closed with respect to its own primitive terms.

The same goes for the axioms: they may be theorems in some other system, but in this system they are not only unprov*ed,* but unprov*able.* Put the other way around, if a proposition can be deduced from the other propositions of this system, it is a theorem, not an axiom.

The rules of the game are constituted by the logic. This is analogous to the rules of chess: they tell the player what he can and cannot, may and must not, do with the several pieces. Note that the rules are, or may be, peculiar to this particular game. The rules of chess are silent about whether the bishop can be used as a paperweight or whether the pawns can be made of chocolate and eaten after the game. The logic of a particular theory, like the rules of a particular game, need not be "universal".

Thus, the player in the theory game is given the axioms and the rules of inference and away he goes, proving theorems. It is part of the rule (as well as of the spirit) of the game that nothing be a theorem that does not follow strictly from the axioms in accordance with the logic. It is not fair to bring in anything from the "outside" no matter how convinced the player is that it is true, and no matter how much it would help in getting to a theorem that the player wants to prove.

That seems simple enough; unfortunately, it is not as simple as it seems. Take Euclidean geometry for example. "We all know" what is meant by point, line, radius. A point is a little dot, a line is the crack in the floor, a radius is how far it is from the sprinkler to where the grass is dry. But, of course, we also know from our high school study of geometry that a point is not as big as the dot, not even a very small dot; in fact, a point is not any big at all – it is dimensionless. And a line is not that thing on the paper which, under magnification, looks like a splotchy path – a line is just a collection of those dimensionless points.

But as long as we are clear about that, what harm is there in thinking of a point as a dot or of a right angle as the corner of the room? What is wrong is that in so thinking, we may be led to introduce some extraneous, "outside", elements into our thinking about triangles and perpendiculars and tangents and, thereby, be led to believe that we have proved something which in fact we have not.

So the geometer attempts to void his primitive terms of any ordinary meaning. In order not to believe we know something about points and lines that we have not learned from the axioms, the mathematician replaces the word "point" by the nonsense word "furb". "Line" becomes "bool". "A line is a collection of points" becomes "A bool is a collection of furbs". Eventually the process would also replace logical terms such as "collection" by some appropriately neutral term.

A geometrical term like "parallel" is handled as follows:

$Bool_1$ is parallel to $bool_2$=no furb that is an element of $bool_1$
is also an element of $bool_2$

Already one begins to feel the peculiarly geometrical content of the Euclidean system slipping away. And this is precisely what is desired. Pushed to its limit, we end up with a deductive system that means, literally, nothing. It has been emptied of all meaning except that which is given to the undefined terms (and only to the undefined terms) by the axioms (and only by the axioms). This is what Heisenberg meant when he said that scientific (i.e., theoretical) concepts are defined through the axioms.

Such a deductive system, voided of all meaning, is not very interesting or useful. Deducing meaningless propositions from other propositions may be a pleasant game, but most of us believe that mathematics has more to offer than intellectual pastimes – and so it does. In order to make mathematics interesting and useful, it must be given an *interpretation*. Suppose we let "furb" stand for voter, and "bool" for political party. On this interpretation, a political party is a collection of voters, which, whether true or not, at least makes sense. The "axiom of parallels" tells us that through a given voter, parallel to another political party, one and only one political party can be drawn. Obviously such a "mixed" or partial interpretation causes problems. But if we go back to the definition of "parallel to", we find that the axiom of parallels states that "No voter who is a member of one political party is also a member of another political party", which is not a bad start on an axiomatization of American politics.

An interpretation is not, of course, crucial to an axiom system; from a purely logical or formal point of view, it is quite possible to work with an uninterpreted system. Whether or not an interpretation is given, and whether or not any proffered interpretation is interesting or useful is, strictly speaking, irrelevant to a formal system. But it is of considerable interest to the consumers, so to speak, the users, of formal theories. For, in the case of Euclidean geometry, it is the interpretation that enables us to calculate the amount of fertilizer we need for the garden and how much paint it will take to paint the house. It will turn out that interpretations are important for metatheoretic reasons as well, but that will be postponed for a few pages.

For us, the consumers, the logical structure of an axiomatic system is less important that the interpretation: we assume that the mathematician has done his job correctly. But for the mathematician, the producer, the utility of the theory is distinctly less important than its internal, formal properties. What, then, are these internal characteristics of a formal system for which the theorist looks? And why does he look for these? Basically, there are three important properties of formal systems for which the metatheorist looks: consistency, independence, and completeness. These are the formal criteria of an axiomatic system.

1. *Consistency,* or, more accurately, internal consistency, means that no axiom contradicts any other axiom. It is often taken as self-evident that a theory should be consistent: that it is simply a formalization of a constraint we place on any kind of communication. Inconsistent behavior or inconsistent language makes signifi-

cant relationships difficult if not impossible. But there is a more fundamental reason why inconsistency or contradiction is intolerable. The reason is that from a contradiction, any proposition whatever follows. Consider the following argument:

(1) Today is Friday.
(2) Today is not Friday.
(3) Today is Friday *or* I'm a monkey's uncle.

[(3) follows from the fact that "p or q" is true if either "p" or "q" is true; since "Today is Friday" is true (1), it follows that "Today is Friday *or* I'm a monkey's uncle" is true.]

(4) But Today is not Friday (2).
(5) So I'm a monkey's uncle.

[(5) follows from the fact that if "p or q" is true (3), and if "p" is *false* (2), then "q" must be true (5).]

By virtue of the contradiction between (1) and (2), I have managed to prove that I'm a monkey's uncle. Naturally, any proposition whatever could have appeared as the last half of (3) – after the "or". So the little argument is capable of proving anything.

Contradictions in little arguments of this sort are not difficult to spot. But when the axiom system is large and complex (such as a system of sufficient power to generate arithmetic), it is by no means obvious when a contradiction lies concealed in the axioms. And if there should be an inconsistency somewhere, every theorem is suspect. A theorem *T* might remain a theorem if the consistency were removed; but then again we might have been able to prove *T* only because of the inconsistency. Thus, as long as the consistency of the system is in doubt, all theorems are in doubt.

In practice, contradictions are not rooted out by inspecting the axioms to see if they contain sentences like (1) and (2) above. The test (which is not the same thing as the definition) of consistency is to give an *interpretation* of the axiom system – either from the "real world" or from another theory, where the latter is presumed (or has been shown) to be consistent. The interpretation constitutes a "model" of the theory in question. Hence the importance of interpretation and model for metatheory.

2. *Independence* is the requirement of non-redundancy. Actually, there are two kinds of independence: "primitive independence" and "postulate independence" (see Bunge, 1972, pp. 240-241). Primitive independence simply means that no term or concept fundamental to the theory is definable by other terms or concepts of the theory.

Postulate independence means that none of the axioms is really a theorem, i.e., that no axiom can be proved on the basis of the other axioms. No logical damage is done if a system is redundant, and sometimes (particularly for pedagogical purposes) it is helpful to work with a redundant system. It is just not a very "clean" system, and this suggests, of course, that independence is as much an aesthetic criterion as anything else.

However, this is not altogether the case. The practical importance of the criterion of independence arises when, for some reason, a theory needs to be fixed up. Bunge comments: "If one wishes to subject a theory to repairs, one has to proceed step by step, and this is possible only if the replacement of any given axiom system by another formula does not force changes in all the others: an independent axiom system is one that does not reject transplants" (1972, p. 241).

3. Finally the *completeness* criterion specifies that every statement (or its denial) expressible in the language of the system be provable as a theorem. Another way of stating this is that the set of axioms contain all propositions that are stable in the language of the theory and that are not theorems of the system. In still other words, no new axioms can be added. A moment's reflection is sufficient to convince one that these are equivalent formulations.

What is the importance of completeness? The theorist wants a theory that is adequate for the job to be done. If he can state things in the language of his theory, but his theory is not powerful enough to prove whether those statements are true or false, the theory is inadequate. There are holes in the theory; not holes in the sense of inconsistencies, but holes which are of such a nature that the theorist must say, "I don't know – my theory won't tell me". He is like the plumber who identifies the problem and knows how to fix it, but finds that his tool kit is inadequate. The plumber needs additional tools; the theorist needs additional axioms.

These are the three central metatheoretical criteria of an internal or formal nature. Bunge suggests a fourth, *viz.*, decidability: the existence of a procedure for deciding whether any candidate statement is in fact a theorem or not. He observes that "the vast majority of mathematical (hence scientific) theories are undecidable", but that this "constitutes no real limitation on the possibility of axiomatizing any branch of knowledge" (1972, p. 242). We will, therefore, disregard the issue of decidability.

In commenting on the lack of a decision procedure, however,

Bunge makes an illuminating and thought-provoking observation that may serve as a bridge from our consideration of the internal/ formal, to the external/factual metatheoretical criteria.

> Moreover, the non-existence of a decision procedure does not preclude admitting or rejecting any particular formula as a member of a given theory T, by using means obtained outside T . . . This is, after all, the way proofs and counterexamples are usually constructed in non-formalized mathematics, namely, with the help of auxilliary constructions and notions borrowed from other chapters of mathematics. Surely by proceeding in this way, the crust of a formalized theory is pierced, but everything proceeds within the self-imposed bounds of reason. Reason cannot be confined within one theory or even within one arbitrarily demarcated field. Every formalism is artificially separated from all the other theories. *Inventive reason puts together what formalizing reason puts asunder.* (1972, p. 243; my italics)

One of the difficulties with logical positivism (the Received View) was its dogmatic insistence on formal scientific procedure as a touchstone for rationality, even for meaningfulness. But reason, as Bunge points out, will not be so confined, and the product of "technical reason" (as Tillich called it in the *Systematic Theology*) is to be distinguished from and perhaps even set over against the product of reason in its creative and expansive role. One can, after all, be irrational in the service of logic.

These three criteria, strictly speaking, characterize only formal, axiomatized theories. Is it, therefore, unsuitable to consider these criteria in application to theories that are *not* fully formalized? What would such an application amount to in the case, say, of a demographic theory in sociology or a theory of diffusion in anthropology? It is certainly not too much to ask that they be consistent. Such theories will make use of a language that is enormously more complicated than even the most elaborate mathematics – for it is one of the advantages of mathematics that it can arbitrarily build its own language; sociology and anthropology do not have that luxury. Thus, the question of consistency will not be as simple as it is in an axiomatized mathematical theory, and even there, as we have seen, judgements of consistency cannot be made by mere inspection of the axioms. And is it not the case that we test the consistency of an anthropological theory by looking at the human societies and cultures which the theory purports to describe to see whether the description is borne out? But this is clearly the analog of what, in formal axiomatics, we call the interpretation of the theory.

And what would the criterion of independence mean for an anthropological or economic theory? Perhaps only that the theorist correctly identify those concepts, peculiar to the field, that are fundamental, in the sense that all other concepts can be derived from them and not the other way around. Is, for example, the avunculate (the remarkable role played by the uncle) in "primitive" societies a primitive concept or is it derivable from other concepts describing the structure of the family? Is the "law of supply and demand" an axiom? Or is it derivable from other propositions (in which case it is a theorem of economics)? This is a demand on the theorist that he make clear the fundamental machinery of his theory, and distinguish that from concepts and principles that are derivative. The importance of independence can be seen when a theory must be modified to account for conflicting or new data. If no distinction has been made between primitive and derivative concepts and principles, the entire theory may have to be dismantled and rebuilt; otherwise one looks for a problem in the primitive terms and axioms which is to be corrected, allowing us to draw the proper theoretical conclusions.

And, finally, completeness. It seems intuitively obvious that any theory in biology or psychology that is unable to respond to questions that can be formulated in the terms of that theory is, to that extent, inadequate and in need of augmentation to fill the holes. Note that this is quite different from a situation in which questions are too difficult, or where the empirical data are lacking. The incompleteness at issue here is one in which the investigator would not even know what sort of evidence to look for in response to the query. "We just don't know enough" covers both kinds of cases; but the metatheoretical criterion is concerned only with the latter.

From this we might conclude that we are justified in holding that the three formal metatheoretical criteria are applicable even to non-formalized or non-axiomatized theories, provided only that we do not ask of those theories more than is reasonable, namely, that we do not require that a non-formal theory behave precisely like a formal one such as mathematics.

D. *Empirical Criteria* In addition to these formal criteria, Bunge (1972, pp. 243 ff.) suggests several other criteria of a factual or empirical nature that apply to scientific, in contrast with purely formal, theories. Such a theory comes with its interpretations built in, as the Received View specified, and is thus already equipped with factual meaning, i.e., the vocabulary of the theory has a specified denotation in the external world to which the theory applies.

The first of Bunge's factual or empirical criteria is (1) *"external consistency* or compatibility with the bulk of corroborated data, hypotheses, and theories" (1972, p. 245). Note that this criterion involves agreement with facts (approximating the old correspondence theory) as well as with the body of theories already accepted. No empirical or factual theory stands alone, but always works in tandem with a host of other theories in the same field and in related disciplines. Thus, for example, a theory in political science dealing with voting behavior accepts, tacitly or otherwise, traditions and theories in economics, psychology, history, etc. While each of these is corrigible and while any bit of factual data is challengeable, a scientific theory may not question everything at once, for then it cuts itself adrift from "the normal mode of testing for truth" (Bunge, *loc. cit.*).

2. *Scrutability* is the requirement that all propositions of a scientific theory be testable, if only indirectly (recall our example of the way in which we test propositions about black holes). To this we need to add the subcriterion of falsifiability: if a body of empirical data (e.g., teen-age promiscuity) is compatible with both of two mutually exclusive hypotheses, (e.g., incest *vs.* sex-taboo in the family), then something is wrong with the theory. This was precisely the issue in the debate over the falsifiability of religious assertions (in Flew and MacIntyre, 1955). If the garden in the wilderness clearing is tended by a gardener who is invisible, who passes freely through walls, who is unaffected by electrical charges, etc., etc. – if the gardener is in principle undetectable by any means whatever – does the gardener hypothesis differ one iota from the hypothesis that no gardener exists? This is a matter to which we will return in our discussion of theories in theology.

3. *Predictive* and *explanatory* power are considered separately by Bunge, because "predictive power is not essential and, even when possessed by a theory, predictive power is not enough: we want every theory to explain the facts in some domain" (1972, p. 246). Nevertheless, as we will see, the ability of a theory to predict is part of the explanatory power of the theory, even though it is not the whole of that explanatory power. Therefore, I will consider these two together under the single criterion of *explanatory power:* the requirement that a scientific theory explain its domain to us.

The reduction of explanation to prediction has been argued

forcibly and influentially by the distinguished Received-View philosopher, Carl Hempel (see, for example, Hempel and Oppenheim, 1953). Commenting on this position Hanson (1971, p. 41) says, "Explaining x is predicting x after it has actually happened . . . Predicting x is explaining it before it actually happened". Thus, in the Hempel view, predicting and explaining are indissolubly linked. It is, of course, true that our understanding of a phenomenon is advanced by learning what it is that causes that phenomenon. If we ask for an explanation of a loud percussion, we expect to be told a story (e.g., about an airplane breaking the sound barrier, or an electrical discharge in the atmosphere, or the demolition of a nearby building) which is such that had we known the story beforehand, we could have predicted the bang.

But does such a story, and the predictability of the bang, exhaust what we mean by an explanation? In a whimsical parody of the Hempel view, "How to succeed in prediction without ever explaining anything", Hanson calls our attention to the fact that theories are not *"mere* predicting devices" (1971, p. 48). Thus, for example, the problem with the theory of behaviorism in psychology or economics or political science is that even though we may be able to predict the behavior of an individual or a social group, we may still feel that we do not understand that individual or group. What more is required?

Bunge says: "A theory accounting for the behavior of its referents, without disclosing what makes them tick, can be a good scientific theory but it is not the best possible theory" (1972, p. 246). We may be able to give a behaviorist account of how a segment of the voting public votes, but such an account will not disclose *why* that is so, that is, what makes those voters "tick". In answer to that question, we expect to be told something about their economic situation, their historical alliances, their self-concept, and so on. These are the kinds of factors that explain why a voting bloc votes as it does. In explaining individual behavior, we think that we understand, or understand better, when we learn about that individual's personality structure, family background, cultural milieu, education, etc.

What this means is that even the ability to predict must go beyond mere statistical correlation if we are to claim to understand the phenomenon. The statistical fact that a lack of fluorine in the diet is associated with a high incidence of tooth decay may be enough to persuade us to fluoridate our water, but it could hardly be said to constitute an *explanation* of tooth decay. What is required in addition is the ability of scientific theory to set the phenomenon to be explained, the *explanandum,* into a wider context in order to demonstrate the relationship between the *explanandum* and the network or pattern of other phenomena surrounding it.

So the voting behavior of urban blacks is explained when we have told the story of their historical alienation from centers of power, their economic deprivation, their low self-concept, and so on. We are said to have explained the delinquency of this youth when we have described his fractured family relationships, his ghetto culture in which crime and violence is a norm, his intellectual and educational deprivation, etc. In each case, the question is not what *causes* what, or how we can *predict* (although these may *also* be involved) but, do we see the wider picture or pattern of which the *explanandum* is an element? A phenomenon *is* just the particular intersection of the network of which it is an element, so that when we have understood the network, the pattern, we have, *ipso facto,* understood that which was to have been explained.

It seems to me very difficult to say anything very sensible about explanation beyond this rather intuitive notion. Understanding something is like getting the point of a joke – given the pattern of the joke, I either get the point or I don't, but *further* explanation is not going to help. The metaphor of drama may clarify this. When I go to a play by Mr Albee, I may see the point he is trying to make, and then again I may not. In the latter case, I leave the theatre shaking my head and saying, "I didn't understand the character of Grandma". I may have read the play beforehand and could, therefore, have predicted what Grandma was going to do at every moment. Still, I don't understand: I have not grasped the pattern in such a way as to *see* what Grandma's role in it is. In Hanson's language, I have not *seen* Grandma *as* the participant in the drama that Albee had intended.

Getting the point, understanding something, may be much more a matter of experience and familiarity than it is having a theory about something. This accounts for the amused tolerance with which the experienced businessman views the junior executive fresh out of Business School. The latter, despite his up-to-date education, is not likely to be able to teach anything more than new techniques to his elder. Experience and familiarity provide a depth of understanding that "mere book-learning", i.e., mere theory, cannot.

But the partnership of wise experience and fresh theory will be better than either taken by itself. Warning us against supposing that we must choose between the two, Hanson points out that it is perfectly possible to enunciate theories that will have the predictive power necessary to satisfy the Hempel criterion, and will also locate the phenomenon to be explained "within an intelligible framework of ideas". Copernican astronomy, Newtonian physics, and the germ theory of disease are surely cases in point. To elaborate such a theory "is to have *explained* the phenomenon in question in the fullest sense modern science can provide" (1971, p. 48).

E. *Pragmatic Criteria.* 1. The *utility* of a theory is sometimes regarded as a matter of indifference so far as the merits of the theory *per se* are concerned. Still, a theory from which one can infer conclusions that are translatable into practical means of dealing with our environment is, *ceteris paribus,* preferable to one that confers fewer such practical benefits.

As already observed, theories are not usually constructed in abstraction from the empirical characteristics of the world they are designed to explain. But they might be. In this respect, the two sides of the world/theory coin are quite different. That facts are theory-laden seems to be a matter of epistemological necessity; the world *cannot* be observed except through the spectacles behind the observer's eyes. But on the other hand, there is no *necessity* that theories be constructed in accordance with the experienced characteristics of the world. That is, it would be *possible* to construct theories out of undefined terms and unproved propositions without regard for the world that the theories were supposed to help us to understand. But if such were the case, it is quite obvious that if a theory explained anything, it would be a matter of the merest accident. The satisfaction of the pragmatic criterion of utility is, therefore, a consequence of the fact that theories are constructed in just such a way as to be useful. Theories are useful because we make them so.

2. Finally, a mere observation that the aesthetic qualities of theory constitute a metatheoretical criterion. Again, other things being equal, the simpler theory is better than the more complex and cumbersome. It is more elegant, as mathematicians say of transparently simple proofs. There are practical reasons for seeking a simple theory, of course: it is easier to get into our heads, and the chances

of our being misled by extraneous considerations are diminished. Still, even without those practicalities, we would, on purely aesthetic grounds, prefer the simple to the complex. This factor may also be related to our conviction that underlying the manifold of experience, there must be a few simple constituents of the world, and a few simple laws that connect those constituents. Thus, a simple theory seems to display the simplicity that we almost instinctively believe to underly the complexity of our ordinary experience.

What is it for a theory to be "simple" is not itself entirely a simple question; but we would surely want to include such considerations as the fewest primitive terms, the least ornate relationships between the primitive terms of this theory and those of other theories, the number of axioms, and so on. (For an illuminating discussion of this issue, see Achinstein, 1971, pp. 11 ff.)

We must not treat these pragmatic criteria (utility and aesthetics) as irrelevant or merely incidental to the *real* metatheoretical criteria. There is a certain analogy, for example, between the theological debate over the bodily assumption of the Virgin and her elevation to the status of co-redemptrix, and the scientific disagreement over Ptolemaic and Copernican astronomy. If the Copernican theory of the solar system can explain everything that the Ptolemaic can and can do so with fewer of the puzzling epicycles that are required to explain such things as retrogradation of planetary orbits, then Copernicus is to be preferred over Ptolemy. And if religion can get along with a Trinity – Father, Son, and Holy Spirit – why do we need a fourth – Holy Virgin? But always with the qualification, *ceteris paribus.*

This is nothing other than the claim that the pragmatists made: if there is no essential superiority of one theory over another on grounds either of coherence or correspondence, then what is so offensive about saying that this theory is true if it satisfies us on "passional" grounds (James, *The Will to Believe*)? That is, *ceteris paribus,* if this theory is simpler and/or more useful than that, what is so bad about saying that this theory is the correct one?

We have cursorily surveyed a large territory, the exploration of which is, of course, a vast undertaking. I have suggested that in determining what a theory is and what makes a theory a good theory, there are four distinct sets of criteria:

Constitutive, as represented in the Received View;
Formal, as comprised by the metamathematical criteria;
Empirical; and
Pragmatic.

In concluding, I suggest that it might be an interesting exercise for the reader to run over these criteria in his mind to see whether and to what extent they apply to other human activities: art, music, poetry, philosophy, personal and social relationships, morality, etc. If they do, and to the extent that they do, these criteria may come close to specifying what it is to be "rational" in each of these areas. These criteria, I suggest, may in fact be a skeleton of what could be called, rather pretentiously, a general theory of value.

Without opening up such a vast terrain, we will look only at the way in which these criteria apply to the theory of religion: the science of theology. This is our central purpose, and to this task I turn next.

CHAPTER III

Religion and Theology

Theology is the *logos* of the *theos*: it is thinking about God. But God is what we worship, pray to, tremble in fear of, rejoice in the love of, anguish over the death of – in short, God is that with which religious experience has to do. It is this that distinguishes the God of Abraham, Isaac, and Jacob from the God of the philosophers. I assume here that religious experience is taken seriously. If not, if someone is persuaded that all "religious experience" is a kind of hallucination, or illusion, or is the result of deceit, then, of course, there is no point in talking about theology, for theology will have no subject matter.

It is not my purpose to offer some kind of "proof" that religious experience is genuine; indeed, I think it neither possible nor necessary to do so. It is not possible for exactly the same reason that it is not possible to prove that our experience of the world is genuine or veridical, namely, that it is meaningless to assert the opposite. To say that a particular experience – a remembered event, or something perceived – is illusory makes sense only because we know what it is to have a *non*-illusory experience, and because we know how to distinguish between illusory and veridical. But to assert that *all* experience is illusion is meaningless, since in so asserting we have cut ourselves off from any evidence whatever that would make it possible to test for illusion. "Vanity, vanity, all is vanity!" is paradoxical at best, since in order to maintain that X is vain there must be at least one Y that is not vain against which to check the vanity of X.

In the same way, it makes sense to say that this particular alleged mystic experience was an hallucination, that that particular feeling of being forgiven was the result of auto-suggestion. But to say that *all* "religious" experience is illusory is to reject from the outset any criterion against which to test a particular alleged instance of religious experience. In the face of such a rejection, there is nothing at all to be said for or against the veridicality of any claim to religious experience, and, *a fortiori,* no proof is possible.

Fortunately, no proof is necessary anyway. For the sense of "proof" that is at issue here is, I presume, the same sense in which we ask whether there is *really* a pink elephant on the piano, or whether its appearance is only an alcohol-induced hallucination. But an examination of religious experience will shortly indicate that religious experience is not that kind of experience, or at least not *typically* that kind of experience, and certainly not *exclusively* that kind of experience. What generates the demand for proof, in the pink-elephant sense, is the mistaken belief that there is some unique kind of experience called "religious", and the further identification of that with mysticism.

Naturally, if a person claims to see God, or hear God, or be touched by God, it makes perfectly good sense to ask whether that perception or sensation was or was not hallucinatory. The answer to the question may not be entirely simple. We would want to determine whether and to what extent the claim fits reports of other mystic experiences, how and whether it fits with other experiences, religious and non-religious, of this particular individual, whether the quality of the experience claimed is consistent with our other ideas of God, and we would certainly want to ascertain something of the mental and even physical condition of the person making the claim. If, for example, as occasionally happens, a man kills his children allegedly under orders from God, we are entitled to be entirely sceptical. Our scepticism would not be the result of any doubt that the man had some experience that led him to think that God ordered him to murder his children. That, we would probably grant. Our doubt, as Christians, would most likely arise out of the fact that what God allegedly told this man to do bears no resemblance to other things that we – and all other Christians – believe and have always believed about God: that he desires not the death of (even) a sinner, that he commands that we love one another, and so on.

I am suggesting that we do not attempt to prejudge the matter by saying that all or no mystic experiences are hallucinatory, or that there is some simple litmus test by which to sort out the real from the illusory. What instead I want to maintain is, first, that experiences of an allegedly religious nature deserve to be considered on their merits, and, second, that it is illegitimate to define religious experience in terms of mysticism, to "dispose" of mysticism somehow, and to conclude that the entirety of religion has thereby been shown to be illusory.

In connection with this second point, we need to be reminded occasionally by William James, in *The Varieties of Religious Experience* (1902), that religious experience comes in a wide range of shapes and sizes. The fiery vision of the mystic takes its place alongside the more modest "sense of the numinous" (Otto) and the "ontological awareness of the unconditional" (Tillich) as candidates for religious experience.

A. RELIGIOUS EXPERIENCE AND ULTIMATE CONCERN

In fact, we may find it helpful in talking about religious experience to think in terms of the religious *dimension* of experience, rather than the religious experience *per se*. The former locution steers us away from the attempt to identify a unique *kind* of experience that we can call religious. The religious dimension has been characterized in a number of ways: a sense of awe, a sense of oneness with the world, the dimension of depth, the awareness of the unconditional, the sense of the numinous, of the *mysterium tremendum,* etc. Running through all these is a common thread: we call an experience *religious* when the experience itself is of such significance, is so charged with meaning, that it becomes central to us in such a way that other experiences and other kinds of experiences take their significance from it, live in the light of its luminescence, so to speak. Consequently, because of the quality of the experience itself, the *object* of the experience is invested with ultimate value and significance, as underlying and giving substance to all else.

I use the expression "religious experience" in this way because it begs the fewest questions. The sense of ultimacy does not commit me to a belief that there is something out there that is ultimate. Indeed, as Tillich contended, I can invest anything with ultimacy: that is why money, sex, power, drugs, science, even religion itself can become "God". To be sure, Tillich says (1957, p. 12) all faiths so grounded are idolatrous, but they are still religious faiths in the full sense, grounded in what Tillich calls "ultimate concern". The state of being ultimately concerned, the "faith state", as James called it, is a clearly recognizable and undeniably real state, regardless of whatever questions might be raised about the object of the ultimate concern or that to which the faith is directed.

The faith state, yielding religious experience, is thus the analog of our ordinary experience of the world. Just as my experience of the clam and the star and my anxiety are in some way unchallengeable, so is my sense of ultimacy as I address myself to the objects of my concern. The critic may take issue with any assertion to the effect that the *object* of my concern is itself ultimate – knowledge, for example, or power – but the critic is no more entitled to dispute the ultimacy of my *concern* than he is to say that I don't really have a feeling of anxiety.

This is not to say, of course, that a faith state cannot be simulated, and indeed, one suspects that protestations of faith sometimes are made in order to persuade others, for some reason or other, that a religious conviction exists where in fact there is none. Nor is it even to say that one cannot under certain circumstances be misled by some psychological state (e.g., loneliness or fear or a severe toothache) into believing quite genuinely that one's concern is ultimate, only to find that the sense of ultimacy disappears along with the psychological state that generated it (e.g., when the tooth is extracted). However, the more important criticism that is levelled at religious experience so understood is that those in whom such experience is manifested are (frequently, at any rate) mentally unbalanced in some way. Religious experience can, therefore, be dismissed from any serious consideration except insofar as it constitutes a symptom of an unfortunate mental aberration. It should perhaps not come as a surprise that certain kinds of mental illness are associated with religious experience as here defined. The powerful, even overpowering, experiences of, say, the schizophrenic, demand some kind of accounting, and it is quite natural that such an account be given in terms of that which is perceived by the schizophrenic to be ultimate.

The question at issue has to do with what we can infer from this with respect to the validity or meaning or value or, indeed, the truth of religious experience. The answer to the question is that we can infer precisely nothing. To infer something about the value or validity of an experience from the psychological state of the person who has the experience is to commit what has come to be known as the "genetic fallacy". And it *is* a fallacy: as the American theologian, A. T. Mollegen, once remarked, it may just be the case that it is the cracked people who let the light through. Certainly no one would want to devalue art or music or poetry because artists and musicians and poets tend to be mentally dishevelled (which is highly dubious). Similarly, any statistical correlation between the occurrence of religious experience and mental illness would prove exactly nothing about the value or validity of religious experience.

Thus, leaving aside mere dissembling or out and out prevarication, there is no reason for us to be concerned with the psychological antecedents or concomitants of religious experience. But its effect on the person is another matter. Anyone who has had a religious experience, no matter how low-key, knows fully how important and moving that experience is. Most of us, I suppose, recall an experience from childhood when we lay on our backs on a summer night gazing up at the stars and were overcome by a deep and ineffable feeling of oneness with the world. We may have had similar feelings of the fundamental rightness and power and beauty of the world when contemplating a work of art or absorbed in a piece of music. Such experiences refer beyond themselves and beyond the occasioning object – the stars, the painting – to that "more" of the universe to which James referred (1902 p. 508). I am suggesting this common sort of experience as a model or prototype of religious experience. If a person can genuinely say that he or she has never had such an experience, that such a prototype awakens no hint of recognition, then I suppose there is nothing whatever to be said by or to such a person about religious experience. It would be exactly like trying to discuss the experience of music with a person who is stone deaf.

B. RELIGIOUS EXPERIENCE, RELIGION, AND THEOLOGY

If we *do* recognize this kind of experience, however, we will surely also agree that it is a powerfully moving experience, and that we want to repeat it, or to have other experiences like it, that we want to tell others about it, to share it with others, to try to get others to have like experiences. We may be led to enshrine the experience in some kind of memorialization. We may search for a peculiarly apt language in which to express it – a language whose power to move is consonant with the moving power of the experience itself. But what has just been described is *religion*. Bible, liturgy, church, canons, laws, meditation, prayer, art, architecture – the whole array of words, artifacts, and practices of religion are nothing other than an attempt to comprehend, express, repeat, extend, and share our religious experience. Critics of religion – particularly, critics of the church – ought never to forget that no matter how silly, trivial, banal, mendacious, even pernicious the church in its present and historical state may be or have been, underlying it is the *mysterium tremendum*: the powerful, shaking experience that we call religious.

It is a pity that so much energy has been invested in "philosophy of religion" when what is much needed is a philosophy of the *religious*. If, instead of beginning with an examination of the proofs for the existence of God, the old war horse of philosophy of religion, we began with a philosophical study of religious experience, out of which has grown such things as the intellectualization of the presumed object of that experience, we would spare ourselves much irrelevant or ineffectual argumentation. There is much to be done in a careful and systematic examination of the religious dimension of our lives; but arguing whether God exists or whether Christians are better or worse people than non-Christians is not the way to do it.

Once the edifice of religion has been erected on the basis of religious experience, that edifice is itself the means for stimulating new religious experience. For example, who has not been religiously moved by the architecture of a great church or by the sonorous poetry of the King James Bible? Religion also acts in a formative way to structure religious experience: to provide a linguistic, conceptual, and social framework within which putative religious experience finds its place. If such an experience fails to fit the accepted structure, it is likely to be devalued or discredited. Thus, in a highly liturgical setting, mysticism may find acceptance difficult; in an evangelical climate, ritual may be viewed with distrust.

So there appears to be an intimate relationship between religious experience and religion: the latter grows out of the former, generates new religious experience, and structures both old and new. But it must be kept in mind that religion is not the same as religious experience. Similarly, religion must not be confused with theology.

The terms are used loosely and sometimes with unfortunate effect. Thus we speak of religious disagreements when we really should be talking about theological disputes; we talk about theological views when what we mean are religious convictions. For example, to say that God created the world in six days, is not to utter a piece of theology; it is rather to assert a religious dogma. On the other hand, to say that "in Him (Jesus Christ) . . . the One Truth of God comes to us in creaturely form and existence" (Torrance, 1969, p. 150) is not to make a religious affirmation, despite the "religious" language, but to propound a theological doctrine.

This is not just a matter of cleaning up our terminology. The reason that it is important to keep the religious separate from the theological is that there are different kinds of warrants or justifications for the two kinds of statements. To conflate the two is to fall prey to the egregious error of supposing that religious affirmations can be rationally established and that theological propositions are justified by supernatural revelation or are the result of enthusiasm. Neither of these is true.

Let us try to sort things out in the following way. First, *religious experience* is, or is indissolubly linked with, the state of being ultimately concerned. It is the state of a person, and is therefore the experience of a person, precisely in analogy with a person's experience of a star or a feeling of anxiety. *Religion* is the crystallization of religious experience into a structure of words, concepts, artifacts, people, and social relationships.

What is characteristic of both religion and religious experience (and the reason why there is no such thing as *the* religious experience) is that they cut across the whole personality. There is a religious dimension, a dimension of depth, to our moral, emotional, social, intellectual, and artistic experience. The entire person – the affective and intellectual, the individual and social being – participates in the religious and in religion. Contrary to some popular views, religion is not a matter of the emotions or of the feelings; neither is it a matter of the intellect. To approach religion as if it could be reduced to one of these – or to some other particular aspect of our lives, such as the social or the aesthetic – is seriously to misunderstand religion and the religious. The misunderstanding is the source of a great deal of fruitless wrangling about religion.

But religion and the religious are problematic. What is a "valid" religious experience? What formulas or texts most adequately express religious experience? What ecclesiastical structures best serve the religious dimension? What is the meaning of religious utterances? How do we tell which are true and which are false? If religion were only an emotional phenomenon, such issues would never arise. But because religion is an intersection of the affective and the intellectual, we cannot help but raise them. Consequently, to answer them, we have to move up the stack one notch above the level of religion (where "above" does *not* mean "superior to").

By virtue of this need to respond to questions about religion and religious experience, *theology* comes into being. Theology is a purely intellectual discipline, just as intellectual as biology or astronomy or anthropology. But if this is so, why can we not dispense with theology and move at once to philosophy in order to address such problems as we have noted? Or to psychology? Or sociology? What is it that distinguishes the intellectual activity of theology from these other disciplines?

The answer is that theology, although purely intellectual, is also *confessional*. This means that the theologian is either a Christian theologian or a Buddhist theologian or a Jewish theologian. There is no such thing as a theologian who is neutral with respect to the religious tradition about which he theologizes. On the other hand, philosophy and psychology and sociology are by their very nature uncommitted in any religious sense. (But note that they may be committed in some other sense; the psychologist may be a Freudian or the philosopher an Hegelian.) The idea of a Christian philosophy is simply self-contradictory, although the idea of a philosopher who is a Christian is by no means contradictory. The very concept of philosophy is violated by the notion of a philosopher who sets out to reflect philosophically about religion, but does so on the basis of the pre-acceptance of a religious tradition that is to form part of the object of his philosophy. There cannot be *ex parte* philosophy.

Finally, it might be observed that the occasional tendency to conflate religion with philosophy is also a mistake. It is sometimes said, for example, that Christianity is a noble philosophy, or something of the sort. But Christianity, for reasons given in the preceding paragraph, is not a philosophy, noble or otherwise. It is important that we keep in the backs of our minds the distinctions and relationships between *religious experience, religion, theology,* and *philosophy,* as well, of course, as the special sciences, such as psychology and sociology.

C. LANGUAGE AND RELIGION

The fact that we use the same words in expressing our religious convictions, our faith, and in our theologizing about that faith is probably one of the reasons we tend to mix up religion and theology. Ordinary language employs many of the words of mathematics and scientific theory, and these words acquired their technical meanings from and in the theory, not in and from ordinary experience. For example, we talk about the shape of our flower-garden as elliptical. "Ellipse" is a geometry word, not a flower-garden word; but ordinary language has appropriated "ellipse" and it is now part of both the theoretical (i.e., mathematical) and the observational (ordinary) vocabulary. The same is true of words such as *ego, nuclear, momentum, acculturation,* and *feedback*. Few people who use the word *feedback* have the slightest acquaintance with cybernetics or the theory of automata. Nevertheless, the word *feedback,* like other theory-words, has the meaning it has because of the theory in which it is technically defined. Ordinary language uses the word ordinarily, i.e., without reference to a theoretical system; theory uses the word theoretically, i.e., in the sense defined by the Received View – as part of the set of primitive terms or as defined by those primitive terms.

Words like God, Salvation, Sin, Redemption, Grace, and Atonement function this way in religion and in theology. Thus, we pray to God without thereby committing ourselves to a theory about what God is; the theologian tries to understand God's nature without thereby addressing entreaties to the object of his inquiries. We ask to be forgiven our sins with no thought about the nature of Sin as alienation or whatever; the theologian reflects on the concept of Sin without feeling particularly alienated or sinful. So the words, and the concepts for which the words stand, function quite differently in religion and in theology.

Sometimes to keep these two senses separate, we adopt the convention of capitalizing the word, as I did in the previous paragraph. This helps us to remember that *Sin* is not the same thing as a *sin*; the former is a theology-concept and has a technical meaning within a theological structure, while the latter often means something like doing a naughty thing. Names such as God and Jesus are always capitalized, so that we have to adopt other devices to keep before us the fact that "God" is now functioning as a theological term in contrast with some ordinary-language term with a fuzzy meaning (such as kindly-old-man-up-there). "Redemption" is one of those theology-words that has almost no ordinary meaning, despite the fact that it is used in religious settings: apart from its theoretical role, a word like "redemption" seems to have virtually no function at all.

To conclude this little excursion into the difficult question of religious language, it might be noted that all such language – religion-words and theology-words alike – began elsewhere, as did most theoretical language. *Triangle* is "three-angle"; but neither *three* nor *angle* started out as a geometry-word. *Force* is an experience-word that became a physics-word. Occasionally words come into existence for special theoretical purposes with no previous history of any experience-usage. The word *laser*, for example, began its life as an acronym, but now has an independent existence; the words of which *laser* is an acronym have receded into the background.

Words like *salvation, redemption, trinity, judgement, grace, holy* – even *God* – came into being from sources that had nothing in particular to do with what we would call religion. The word *God* began its life as a verb, not a noun, meaning something like the activity of calling or invoking. Such ordinary-language words were appropriated by religion when they were used to characterize a state of affairs that was felt to manifest the dimension of depth or ultimacy. And they became theology-words when they were set into and given their theoretical meaning by the theoretical system constituting a theology. This is the linguistic analog of our saying that there is no peculiarly religious experience to which peculiarly religious words apply, but rather that religious experience is merely ordinary experience invested with the dimension of ultimacy (cp. James, 1902, Ch. 2). Religion-words do not constitute a peculiar vocabulary, but become the language of religion by participating in the ultimacy with which the experience to which they apply is invested.

D. DATA AND FACTS IN THEOLOGY

What it means to say that theology is theory which has religion and the religious as its subject matter will be discussed in more detail in the next chapter. At the appropriate point, I will explain how the Received View provides a model for theology, as it did for theory in science. For the time being, I will ask that the reader

accept provisionally the appraisal of theology as an intellectual discipline whose function is to make religion available to the understanding in the way that scientific theory renders ordinary experience understandable.

If this is accepted, if follows that it is not within the province of theology to *challenge* religious experience. It is the task of theology *in general* to try to make sense of our experience of ultimate concern and of the objects of that experience, now also invested with ultimacy. Theology is not commissioned to decide whether this or that experience is or is not "valid" for me, nor whether the faith confessed by that theology is or is not "true".

It is the task of *Christian* theology in particular to build a consistent picture of what Christians claim to experience as members of the *ecclesia,* of the Church. It is no more the function of Christian theology to offer a critique of Judaism or of psychoanalysis than it is the function of astrophysics to tell us what is wrong with the Christian idea of grace. Theology has a domain, just as any other intellectual discipline has. Its domain is *given* to it, and its purpose is to explain the facts of that domain. It is not to question that domain, nor is it to arrogate to itself some allegedly superior point of view from which to examine critically things that lie outside that domain. What this means for the structure and function of theology we reserve for the next chapter.

But we have already raised the questions of *data* and *facts* in theology. If theology is theory about the religious, then it must operate with certain givens – the data. And if it is to operate in any way analogous to scientific theory (which it is the burden of this book to argue), then, like scientific theory, it must have something to do with the facts. Recalling our discussion of Chapter I, we may already have a sinking feeling that anything recognizable as *facts* in religion will be even harder to come by than they are in the subject matter of the sciences. On the other hand, we may be cheered by our conclusion that although factuality or facticity is not pasted on the surface of the *observabilia* of the world, we did not for that reason find ourselves in a position of having to deny objectivity to the sciences. So perhaps we can be optimistic about our results in theology.

T. F. Torrance in a book entitled *Theological Science* (1969, p. 178) speaks of "the whole *fact* of Christ, as God and Man . . . He is a unique *Fact* in History, the absolute Fact become historical fact" (my italics, Torrance's capitals). Later, Torrance says, "It must not be forgotten that the sole Object of dogmatic statements is the Datum of divine Revelation" (p. 351). Only the person who has been hypnotized by capitalized words could fail to sense that there is something odd going on here. The facts to which Torrance points, the data involved in his account of theology are certainly not like any facts or data that any scientist talks about. What *is* going on here?

First we have to distinguish between data and facts. Data are things that are given to an investigator for the purposes of his investigation. Data, therefore, do not float around in some kind of neutral intellectual space; rather, we call something a datum when and only when it is assigned some appropriate role in some theory. From this it follows that not all facts are data; indeed, most facts (e.g., that I have a blister on my heel) never appear in any theory whatever and therefore never serve as data for any inquiry.

It also follows that although something may serve as a datum in one theory it will not necessarily serve as a datum in any other theory. The time of the transit of Arcturus on a particular day may be a datum for an astronomer, a navigator, and an astrologist, but it is not a datum for the chemist, the biologist, or the psychologist (although my belief *that* Arcturus crosses the meridian at midnight could conceivably be of psychological importance).

From this, finally, it follows that the ability of something D to function as a datum in some theory does not depend on the truth status of a proposition asserting D. Data may thus comprise hypotheses, conjectures, observational reports, results of other inquiries, etc. To say that D is given (as a datum) is not to say that it is given *truly*. That is why data must be distinguished from facts. While it would be quixotic to talk about false facts or facts that were wrong, it is not the least inappropriate to describe the data of some study as being in error. Data can be false; facts cannot; therefore data and facts are different kinds of things. Not all facts are data, and not all data are facts.

The application to Professor Torrance's assertions is, I hope, clear: even if it is true that the data for dogmatics are given us in divine revelation, it does not follow from that alone that divine revelation or the contents thereof is guaranteed factual status. We will talk about this further when we come to discuss the "dogmatic inversion".

What about facts? Why is it unsettling to be told by Professor Torrance, that Christ as God and Man is a *fact*? One of the reasons is surely that there is a very large number of people who would vigorously dispute the facticity of Christ's being God and Man, not on the grounds that the statement "Christ is God and Man" is false, not because the evidence is not yet sufficient to decide, but because the kind of assertion made in the proposition "Christ is God and Man" is not one that asserts a fact at all. Pushed hard enough, this line of argument may settle down into old-fashioned positivism: if we are unable to specify the observations that would verify, the proposition is meaningless. But I do not want to press the objection in that direction.

Rather, drawing on our earlier discussion, I want to maintain that *God, Christ,* and *Man* (with a capital M) are functioning here as theoretical terms, specifically as theology-words. Those words, and the concepts they stand for, have meaning in a particular theological setting; take them out of that setting, that context, and their meanings change or vanish altogether. There is no neutral, "inter-theological" territory in which words like *God, Christ,* and *Man* can function. The fact that Christ is God and Man is a "fact" that can be stated only in the language of a particular theory.

This is why discussions across religious lines, or between believers and nonbelievers, are so frequently unproductive. My efforts to persuade Albert the atheist of the religious significance of a particular experience I have had is likely to get nowhere because I am constrained to conduct my end of the conversation in a theological language that is *ipso facto* meaningless to Albert. If Albert and I have any significant exchange of views whatever – even a significant disagreement – it will be because my theology has come into contact with Albert's theology, not because my theology has encountered his theory-free point of view. Theology is theory about the religious, and any discussion whose language involves religious meanings implies theology. We can no more take off the spectacles behind our eyes when we talk about religion than we can when we talk about ducks and rabbits, goblets and silhouettes.

E. THEORY-LADEN EXPERIENCE IN RELIGION

Let us shift the emphasis in Torrance's statement. Instead of emphasizing the *fact* of Christ as God and Man, emphasize the fact of Christ *as* God and Man. The *fact* of Christ as God and Man involves our seeing Christ *as* God and Man. The similarity between this and Hanson's "seeing *as*" is too pronounced to be overlooked.

Tillich almost always speaks of Jesus, the Christ, or Jesus, who is the Christ. Why does Tillich carefully separate the name, Jesus, from his title, Christ? The answer is that for the Christian, *seeing* Jesus is *seeing* him *as* the Christ; the Jew does not see Jesus as the Messiah. I am caught up by the power of Jesus' personality as it shines through the New Testament writers; Albert is not. The brotherhood of man fills Albert with awe and zeal; it is a matter of indifference to me. This reminds us of the fact that I can see the figure as a goblet, or I can see it as a silhouette, but I cannot see it as both. Sometimes a biblical passage or a prayer from the Prayer Book moves me deeply – it is the occasion for a religious experience. At other times that same passage or prayer will at most excite a modest interest in its historical origins. And sometimes it may have no meaning at all for me. Sometimes the duckrabbit is seen neither as a duck nor as a rabbit but as a silly scribble.

Professor Torrance, referring again to the fact of Christ as God and Man, says that we are "unable to report the *historical* fact of Christ truthfully without reporting in the mode of *faith*" (1969, p. 178, my italics). One might quibble about the appropriateness of any reference whatever to the historicity of *Christ,* where "Christ" is understood to be Jesus' title. (Could we refer to the historical fact of the President? – or could we only speak significantly about the historical fact of Ronald Reagan, who is the President?) But we must surely endorse the general principle underlying Professor Torrance's proposition: namely, that any historical "fact" whatever, is a fact, or becomes a fact, by virtue of being *seen as* that fact.

A fortiori, this is true of the "facts" of religion about which theology is concerned. The content of my religious experience, and therefore the content of our religions, is formed and shaped by our world-views, our bliks, as well as by our theories in biology, geology, psychology, and, of course, theology itself. Our religious experience, and what we count as the facts in religion, are, in Hanson's phrase, theory-laden. Therefore, when Professor Torrance speaks of the fact of Christ as God and Man, we must be on our guard. For we might find him saying next that if we do not see that Christ is God and Man we are either "spiritually blind" or just obdurate.

As in the case of scientific theory, we must avoid a naive realism in theology. What appears in my religious experience is very much the product of the world-views that I have absorbed since birth and of the theologies in which I have been instructed. The Jew, who fails to see Christ as God and Man, is neither obdurate nor spiritually blind. He simply does not see Jesus *as* Messiah.

This is of the utmost importance. If I do not see the duck in the duckrabbit, it will not help one iota for someone to explain how happy I will be if and when I do. Simply to be told over and over again that there is a duck there to be seen will not help either. Nor will it do any good for someone to beat me with a stick every time I say I do not see the duck. These are all familiar, albeit highly ineffective, devices by which we try to convert the non-believer to our point of view.

F. THEOLOGICAL REALISM

If I am to see Jesus as the Christ, there must be something else, some other data, something about the perceived Jesus in virtue of which I see him as the Christ. In Hanson's language, I *see* Jesus *as* the Christ because I *see that* Jesus has certain characteristics or engages in certain kinds of activities. The theological assertion that Jesus is the Christ therefore entails or pre-supposes a reference to the characteristics and activities of a real person in the real world. I say that Jesus is the Christ because of the empirical facts that Jesus was and said and did certain things.

This argument can be generalized across all of the theoretical vocabulary of theology. Thus, for the same reason that scientific theory finds itself committed to a kind of realism (but not a naive realism), theology would appear to involve a conviction that there are real things and events and activities corresponding to its theoretical terms: God, Christ, Resurrection, Sin, etc. In the same way that science explicates, but does not legislate, our experience of the world, it is the task of theology to explain the meaning of our religious experience, and not to tell us what the content of that experience is supposed to be. Unless theology has real referents in the world, the science of theology will be exactly like the logical games we play with uninterpreted systems, and will therefore do nothing at all toward helping us to understand our religious experience.

In our traditional worship-language, we confess our belief in Almighty God, Maker of Heaven and Earth, and we offer our prayers to that God. A naive realism in theology would, or might, lead us to suppose that God was something like a powerful but very remote craftsman, and that our prayers to him were rather like our petitions to a cabinet-maker with respect to some kitchen cabinets we wanted him to make. But, of course, it is by now universally agreed, at least above the level of Sunday school classes for the very young, that God is not like that. He is not kindly-old-man-up-there or vengeful-curmudgeon. These are pictures of God painted by a simple-minded theology. But we then stand on the brink of an assumption that having put aside that simplistic and naive theology, we can see God as he *really* is. The Eskimo sees the world through his peculiar world-view, but we perceive the world in its true reality. Many of us (including myself) have been vastly impressed by the theology of Paul Tillich with its sophisticated concept of God as the "ground of Being". Precisely because of the great sophistication of such a theological system, it is all the more important that we understand that it offers us yet another set of spectacles through which to survey religion and the religious. Perhaps a *better* set of spectacles, but a set of spectacles, nevertheless. Moreover, Tillich's contention that the proposition "God is being-itself" is a non-symbolic statement (1967, V.I, p. 238) does not dissuade us from this assessment of his – and all other – theology. What might be meant by saying that Tillich's theology is better than some other must be left until a later discussion of metatheological criteria.

As ordinary experience is, as philosophers would say, "normative" for scientific theory, so religious experience is normative for theology. That is, religious experience constitutes the *given* for us. It is the task of theology to explain that experience, and not to tell us that it is something other than what it is. Theology, therefore, stands in exactly the same relation to religious experience as scientific theory does to our ordinary experience of the world. But this carries with it the same *caveat* that we found necessary in scientific theory: we are never in direct and immediate contact with something called the facts, either in ordinary perception or in religious experience. A religious fact is not something that can be stored in the vestry and brought out for each worship service. A fact in religion is, as in science, always a fact *that* something is the case. But what is the case, is what is perceived to be the case. What is perceived to be the case is theory-laden, and, in particular, theology-laden.

Our attention is therefore directed to the internal nature of theology, as it was to the formal metatheoretical criteria in science. That this is so, and its meaning for our assessment of theology, will be the subject of the next chapter.

CHAPTER IV

The Dogmatic Inversion

Our intent is to test the proposition that the metatheoretical criteria discussed in Chapter II are applicable to theological systems as well as to scientific theories and so to buttress the hypothesis that science and theology are not disparate kinds of activities. That will be the topic of Chapter VI. Here, however, we must say more about the nature of theology, what it is and what it does. This is necessary in order that we may see what the internal structure and external reference of theology is, on the basis of which to determine the applicability of what I have called the formal and factual metatheoretical criteria.

I have contended that theology is about religion and religious experience, just as in the sciences we deal with, and attempt to give an accounting of, the contents of ordinary experience. However, this leads us to the same sort of bind with respect to the facts on which theology proceeds, namely, that there are no "religious facts" floating around to be perceived by the "religious consciousness". All "facts" in religion, as in our ordinary observation of the world, are theory-laden (where that term will always be understood sufficiently broadly as to include the loading of observation by our bliks or world-views). As a consequence, the same kind of subjectivity infects theology as we found in science.

Despite its claim to objectivity, science has understood for a very long time that all scientific hypotheses, theories, consequences, predictions, and "truths" are corrigible. No one of them, nor all of them, can be allowed to harden into dogma or be regarded as infallible. On the other hand, it sometimes happens that in order to avoid the all-too-frequent perception of the scientist as some kind of white-coated *guru,* writers bend over backwards to emphasize the tentativeness and fallibility of scientific research. While, to be sure, every proposition of science is *in principle* challengeable, in practice, there are a very large number that are simply not going to be subject to serious question. Apart from the Flat Earth Society, no one does or will challenge the truth that the earth is round, or that we live in a heliocentric solar system. Hence, one ought not to succumb to the temptation to make too much of the perfectly valid principle of corrigibility.

A.   TRUTH CLAIMS IN THEOLOGY

But theology would appear to be in a somewhat different situation. Running through a great deal of theological discourse are claims to Truth, indeed, to final and ultimate Truth. The Christian may be inclined to think of other religious traditions as benign, or perhaps even pernicious, error, arising out of lamentable superstition, or unenlightened cultural norms, or just flat-out mistakes and illusion. Typically and historically Christians have not regarded other religious traditions as commensurate with, and to be taken as seriously as, Christianity. The reason is simple: Christianity is *true,* and the others are in some important sense *false.* Thus, when Professor Torrance says "Jesus Christ is not only the eternal Word and universal Truth of God but he is a concrete individual existent in human history, combining in himself the universal and the particular, truth and existence, God and creaturely man" (1969, p. 182), one does not get the impression that an hypothesis is being tentatively advanced for our consideration.

One must not be misled by a certain fashionable willingness on the part of some Christians to grant the merits of other religious traditions. From the point of view of a person who knows in his heart that he is Right, it is often appealing (in part, because it shows *how* right he is) to smile indulgently at the error of others. At least that is so as long as no real conflict arises. When conflict does arise, however, rightness often turns to righteousness and thence to intolerance of what previously was only innocent error. Bigotry is the last refuge of Rightness under attack.

Leaving aside this perversion of religious conviction, however, we are still left with the question, What is *truth* in the sense requisite to the present discussion? What *is* the truth that Christian theology is about? And what is it to be *right*? What is the Christian right in saying? The issue is clouded by the fact that "theology" is a highly ambiguous term. There are all kinds of theology: pastoral, moral, biblical, philosophical, dogmatic, systematic, apologetic, revealed, natural, etc., etc. It almost seems that anything having something to do with religion tacks onto itself the word "theology", so that "theology" becomes more of an honorific title for some activity than a description of it.

B. THE UNIQUENESS OF THEOLOGY

This suggests that before we try to answer the questions (What is the truth that theology is about? What is the theologian right in saying?) we should perhaps address more fully the question, what is theology? It is, as I maintained in the previous chapter, the effort to understand systematically our religious experience. But "religious experience", as I have used it, is intentionally so general as to mean practically anything, since it encompasses ordinary experience of almost any kind whatever, insofar as that experience is imbued with the sense of ultimacy. Besides, given the sense of ultimacy attaching to our experience, what can the theologian say about it that the psychologist cannot? Indeed, Abraham Maslow's discussion of "peak experiences" (1976) would seem to address itself to just that aspect of our experience. Certainly, the mere fact that a writer devotes attention to the dimension of depth, or the sense of ultimacy in our experience does not turn that person into a theologian. For all of James' discussion of religious experience, he remained a psychologist.

If we are concerned only with the experience of ultimacy, we may have exhausted the topic when we have traced it through its psychological and cultural antecedents and have discovered its impact on persons and cultures. In just the same way, all of our knowledge of the world – scientific and other – could be translated into reports of perceptions and ideas – the furniture of the mind as it contemplates the world – with no reference to what it is that is being contemplated. Such a phenomenological reduction is essentially what happens in the instrumentalist version of the Received View. If we were to adopt an instrumentalist view of theology, we would find theology collapsed into psychology or sociology: its task would be to map the religious experience of a person or culture, to make inferences as to how that person or that culture would respond to certain stimuli (e.g., involvement with other persons or cultures), and to determine whether those inferences were borne out.

Theology, on such an instrumentalist interpretation, would really have nothing to do with God or Jesus or sin or grace, but only with the "interior" aspects of the experience of the person or of the culture which acquire the religious labels "sin", "grace", etc. Theology would become, in fact, a mere phenomenology of religious experience or of religion, or a form of psychological or sociological behaviorism. Any claim by theology to the perception of a truth that escapes the notice of the special sciences, any claim to be able to say something significant in a mode unique to theology, would have to be forfeited. Theology would have been reduced without remainder to psychology and/or sociology.

We want more than that from theology, although there are those critics who do indeed hold that theology has nothing to offer in the way of knowledge or insight. So the question is, what contributions does theology have to make to our understanding of religion and the religious that do not merely duplicate those of psychology or sociology? If we can identify such contributions, then the reduction of theology to psychology or sociology (or any others of the sciences) will have been shown to be in error.

For the same reason that the Received View of scientific theory tends in the direction of a realist, rather than an instrumentalist, interpretation, theology also leans toward the view that there are real things "out there" corresponding to and denoted by the theoretical terms of its vocabulary: things like God, Savior, Sin, Man, etc., and activities like redeeming, saving, healing, etc. The reason that science tends toward realism, it will be recalled, is simply that it is very awkward for the scientist to adopt the position that it is his sole concern to make the *theory* work right, and that the question whether there really was a Big Bang, for example, or whether surplus value is a reality in the economy, is of no interest.

The same is true of the theologian. Insofar as theology contains theoretical terms like God, Savior, judging, redeeming, and so on, the theologian will be hard pressed to turn his back on such questions as whether sin has really been overcome, whether there really is a Savior, and whether the name of that Savior is Jesus. It will be as difficult for the theologian as it is for the scientist to look on the theory as an uninterpreted, formal system, a kind of intellectual game the connection of which to the real world is irrelevant. Theology, like science, is therefore moved in the direction of realism.

After the discussions of the first chapter, it should not be necessary to dwell on the fact that a realism in theology does not imply a *naive* realism. To believe that there is really a superego "in here" does not mean that I believe that there is a little spook inside my head; to believe that there is really a Messiah and that his name is Jesus does not entail a causal theory of salvation, for example. It is not the case that the ontological correlates of the technical terms of the theological vocabulary must correspond to a set of concepts held by any particular person or group of persons.

What can and must be guaranteed, however, is the integrity of religious experience. Scientific theory, whatever *else* it may tell us about the clam and the star, must not deny our ordinary experience of the clam and the star. Similarly, theology is not commissioned to legislate with respect to religious experience. Note that this is not the same thing as saying that religious experience is *independent* of theology. We have already observed the theory-laden character of religious experience; but to say that theology affects, or contributes to, or is in part determinative of the content of religious experience is not to say that it is the function of theology to exercise a *normative* role with respect to that experience – to tell us which religious experiences are and are not "acceptable" or "valid". There is the same kind of intractability, or given-ness, about religious experience as there is about the experience of seeing the goblet in the Köhler figure: we see what we see, and no theory of any kind is empowered to tell me that I do not or ought not to see it.

Keeping that very important *caveat* in mind, we can agree that theology may tell us some things we did not know before and that as a consequence, our ideas of God and Sin and Creation may have to be refined or amended, just as we may have to refine or amend our ideas of a boll-weevil, depending on what the entomologist tells us.

The problem in all of this is the analog of the problem we encountered in Chapter I about the place where theory and world meet. How are we to understand the intersection of religious experience and theology, such that the former retains its normative status with respect to theology, and the latter maintains its theoretical integrity: that is, without collapsing theology into a mere report of religious experience, or without turning religious experience into a mere intellectual exercise?

The answer, in the case of scientific theory, was that observation, empirical experience, does indeed furnish the data for theory, but not in any simple, "photographic", way. Scientific theory is not a kind of intellectual vacuum sweeper that sucks up undigested facts at random for processing in some separate part of the scientific world. There is, instead, a mutuality between facts and theory such that observation, "facts", in the ordinary use of the term, stimulate and guide theoretical activity and provide for verification of theory, while theory structures our observation and the facts that observation produces.

These two sides of the mutuality, when considered in the theological context, generate two modes of theology, depending on whether one focuses on the theoretical, or on the observational, activity. Those two modes are often called *dogmatic* and *apologetic*, respectively. We will have no further need to consider any of the other kinds of theology that I listed a few pages earlier. I want to examine apologetic theology first and then turn attention to dogmatics. It is essential that we be as clear about this distinction as we can be, inasmuch as the application of the metatheoretical criteria developed in Chapter II will depend on the mode of theology to which the criteria are to be applied.

C. APOLOGETICS

"Apologetics" is the systematic effort to justify the religious point of view, Christianity, for example. (From this point onward I will restrict my discussion to Christianity. It exemplifies what I want to say as well as any other religious tradition; it is probably more familiar to the readers of this book, as well as its author, than any other tradition; and if I talk about Christianity and Christian theology, it will save a great deal of rhetoric about religious traditions in general and theology in general.)

The justification of a religious point of view may take the form of an attempt to *prove* that, e.g., Christianity, is *true*. I have no objection to this, provided the words "prove" and "true" are used in a sufficiently broad sense. But if "prove" is used in the pink-elephant sense (that there exists, or there does not exist, a pink-elephant on the piano), and if "true" is used in the narrow,

positivistic sense of empirical verification, then to say that apologetic theology aims at "proving" the "truth" of Christianity will be far
too restrictive. The only acceptable sense of "prove" for my
purposes will be a very broad sense which would include such
considerations as that Christianity or the Christian point of view
helps me to understand my experience, perhaps even helps me to
make sense of my life, better than any alternative point of view that
I am able to consider. On the whole, a more colorless word like
"justify" would seem to be appropriate in this context rather than
the stronger word "prove".

In the kind of justification required by apologetics, the epistemological starting point lies outside the Christian point of view
itself, and the theologian "works his way up" to the justification of
Christianity. At the heart of Christianity lies an affirmation of faith,
a "this I believe", a *credo*. It is the task of Christian apologetics to
display the warrant for the *credo* in the light of other considerations,
i.e., considerations or evidence or factors that are not peculiarly
infected by the Christian point of view itself. The *data* for the
apologetic theologian are, therefore, to be found in experience.
Apologetics is empirical, in an entirely non-special sense of "empirical".

One kind of apologetics is natural theology, in which one begins
with the facts of observation, with the conclusions of the special
sciences (such as biology), and with the data of ordinary experience,
and derives theological conclusions such as the existence and nature
of God, the purposiveness of the world, the probability of immortality, etc. The so-called teleological argument is perhaps the clear-
est example of natural theology at work. Putting the argument in a
simple form, the inference is from the empirical evidence of design
and purpose in the world to the existence of an intelligent, benevol-
ent Designer. Random processes do not produce such extraordinary "tuning" as we find in a watch or a hummingbird. We know
where the watch came from and that it was produced by an
intelligence; can we believe less of the hummingbird? And if the
natural world is, with a high degree of probability, the product of
an intelligence, can we suppose anything other than that all creatures, including ourselves, have a part to play in some cosmic
drama – that the world and all that is in it has a purpose, an end, a
telos toward which it strives?

The argument is a perfectly recognizable and quite respectable
argument in the mode of the natural sciences. But, of course, we

know a good bit more about natural processes than we did in the 18th century when the "design argument" was in its heyday.

Without rehearsing the history of this or any other argument characteristic of natural theology, let it only be said that the whole enterprise of natural theology withered under the sceptical attacks of Hume and his successors, and in the light of extraordinary advances in natural science. In recent years, with the renaissance of dogmatics, several generations of theologians, beginning with Karl Barth, have subjected natural theology to intense criticism (see, for example, the exchange between Barth and Brunner in a fascinating volume entitled *Natural Theology,* 1946).

The upshot of all this is that natural theology is out of fashion. But that should never be supposed to imply that apologetics has been abandoned, for natural theology is only one form of apologetics. A more persuasive form is to be found in the existential theology of Paul Tillich (most notably, in his *Systematic Theology,* 1967). Tillich does not employ the usual arguments (teleological, ontological, etc.). In fact, he maintains that all such arguments are invalid – at the same time insisting that the *question* that calls forth the arguments is a perfectly valid question (1967, V.I, p. 205). For the question is the question of the ground of being – of that which underlies and gives form and substance and power and value to everything that is.

Instead of approaching the question with the machinery of empirical argument (as in the design argument) or on the basis of purely rational, *a priori* considerations (as in the ontological argument), Tillich uses what he calls the "method of correlation" (1967, V.I, pp. 59 ff.). By this he means that in order to justify the Christian point of view, it is necessary to demonstrate that Christian doctrine speaks to our existential concerns. If I am troubled deeply about death, for example, or if I feel alienated from my fellowman and from the natural world, if I experience a sense of guilt over my inability to establish meaningful relationships (all of which are recurrent themes of modern literature and philosophy), my religion either has something significant to say about those experiences or it doesn't. If it doesn't, then however impressive its history, however magnificent its language, however elegant its structure, it is no more meaningful to me and of no greater religious value than a bit of science fiction.

It is the task of the theologian, in Tillich's view, to demonstrate the correlation or to show how Christianity – Bible, Creed, and

Church – speaks to these existential concerns. What, for example, is the meaning of the story of Adam and Eve? Even if it were possible to argue that it is historically factual, what would it say *to me*? Even in the unlikely event that my misfortunes are due to something called Sin, and that my sinful state is traceable genetically to Adam and Eve, the only consequence would be to make me annoyed at my first ancestors. But what might be its *religious* significance? Unless I see the story of the Fall as shedding light on my sinful condition, as helping me to understand that my feelings of guilt and alienation have something to do with *my* wilfulness (not just Adam's and Eve's), that this wilfulness is built into my very nature, and is therefore not to be eliminated by merely trying harder, that – as the New Testament sequel tells us – I am doomed to separation until reconciliation has been effected by the New Adam, by the atoning sacrifice of the Christ – until all of this gets put together in an account of the whole story from Creation to Resurrection, the tale of Adam and Eve remains a merely interesting legend from a faraway place and time. If, after the theologian has done his best to exhibit the existential relevance of the biblical story, we still do not see the point, the matter is at an end. If I do not "get" the joke, all the explaining in the world will not help. But if I *do* get the point of the story of Adam and Eve, of the birth narratives, of the feeding and healing stories, of the miracle stories, and finally of the crucifixion/resurrection story, if these stories in fact help me to sort out and make sense of my experience, then the Christian story, Christianity, has been justified.

This may not be enough for some Christians. Such a justification does not constitute an argument for general religious truths, e.g., that God exists or that we are assured of immortality. The method of correlation does not offer coercive proof, of the pink-elephant variety, of such truths. I will assert (but will not argue) that the Christian is not interested in general "truths" anyway: the truth of the Christian message is a particular truth, not a set of general, philosophical or scientific propositions. Existential theology, the line of which has only been hinted at above, is a way of validating the Christian point of view, and therefore fulfills the mission of theology by demonstrating the way in which we can make sense of our religious experience. Since it rests on an empirical appraisal of experience, it can rightly be called apologetic.

However unfamiliar existential theology may be for most non-theologians, and however problematic it may appear, there is one respect in which the conventional wisdom about religion will agree with the existentialists, and that is in the conviction that the concepts of religion are ultimately grounded in human experience. It seems almost self-evident that our concept of God as Father, or our concept of Love in the sense of *agape* be drawn from our ordinary experience of fatherhood and of loving. Thus – so it would seem – we take our ordinary notion of fatherhood or love and expand it to an indeterminately large size. Such an expansion transforms an ordinary concept into a theological one and we then fit it, along with all other concepts so derived, into a theological theory.

D. DOGMATICS

However self-evident this may seem, it is important to realize that there is nothing at all self-evident about it. If we turn our attention now from apologetics to dogmatics, we will find that the theologian does not do at all what seems so obvious to the conventional wisdom. For example, in commenting on the father-hood of God, Barth says:

> It is therefore not that there is first of all human fatherhood and then a so-called divine Fatherhood, but just the reverse: true and proper father-hood resides in God, and from this Fatherhood of God what we know as fatherhood among us men in derived. (1949, p. 43)

What Barth does here is precisely the reverse of the procedure supposed by the conventional wisdom. Instead of beginning with the idea of human fatherhood and puffing it up to God-size, Barth says that we understand what it is to be a human father by first knowing what is meant by the Fatherhood of God and then applying that knowledge to the human relationship. Do we understand "God's healing grace" by extrapolating from the healing activity of the family physician? No, it is the other way around: if we are to understand the healing mission of the physician, then we must see that mission in the light of the full and true notion of Healing as evidenced in the New Testament healing stories.

This is what I call the *dogmatic inversion,* or the *dogmatic turn.* As Marx said of Hegel, dogmatics finds the conventional wisdom standing on its head and turns it right side up. It is not our ordinary notion of sinning – doing nasty things – that tells us, when suitably expanded, what Sin is; we learn what Sin is about by reading the story of Adam and Eve, and after we learn that theological lesson, we are in a position to understand what it is to do, and what is wrong with doing, nasty things.

One example to illustrate the technique of the dogmatic turn. How do we know that the resurrection took place as a real historical event? Conventional religious wisdom would say that we look at the evidence, just as we would in an effort to determine whether Caesar's crossing the Rubicon were a real historical event. Since we cannot avail ourselves of eyewitnesses and motion pictures and newspaper stories, we have to rely on less satisfactory evidence: what Caesar himself wrote, what other people said in their writings, archaeological evidence, and so on. Similarly, in order to justify the belief in the resurrection, we have to scrape up whatever evidence we can, most of which, unfortunately, is to be found in the Bible. This is unfortunate from the historian's point of view, because the Bible is not exactly a "neutral" historical text.

Insofar as we feel warranted in accepting the historicity of the resurrection on this kind of evidence, conventional wisdom would then put the event of the resurrection into service as justifying further beliefs, such as, for example, the belief that Jesus was indeed the son of God. As we now expect, the dogmatic theologian turns this the other way around. So Professor Torrance says:

> A full positive account of the historical Jesus Christ . . . must include an assessment of His *resurrection* as a real historical event . . . It is indeed from the perspective of the resurrection that the New Testament witness to Jesus is given . . .

So far, this sounds very much like the conventional account. But note now the dogmatic inversion as Torrance continues:

> In the resurrection the saving intervention of God in our human being and His interaction with 'this passing world' overcome the corruption of our existence, redeeming time from its decay and futility, and result in a fully authentic historical happening . . . (1969, p. 335)

I want especially to call attention to the words *and result in*. How do I know that the resurrection was an historical event? What is the evidence for believing it took place in "the same sphere of reality to which we as human beings belong" (loc. cit.)? The warrant for this belief is not ordinary historical evidence, but is the conviction that the resurrection is the result of "the saving intervention of God". The historical resurrection is not, therefore, to be used as "proof" of "the saving intervention of God" as the conventional view would have it; instead, it is our independent knowledge of God's action in the world that supports and warrants our belief in an historical resurrection.

But where does our knowledge of God's saving intervention come from? That is clearly a theoretical construct. The phrase "the saving intervention of God" is not an article of any creed, nor is it a passage from the Bible. It is, rather, a theoretical term appearing in a particular theory, i.e., in a theology that has been constructed by Professor T. F. Torrance, for the purpose of systematizing and rendering more understandable the Christian faith.

But the Christian faith must have something to so with my religious experience; otherwise, I would not be a Christian. However, I have certainly not experienced any resurrection, to say nothing of anything I would have called "the saving intervention of God". What is the experience that this term – and the theological system in which it occurs – is supposed to refer to and illuminate? To what data does Professor Torrance appeal as justifying the introduction of this theoretical construct, "the saving intervention of God", on the basis of which he then believes it possible to warrant a belief in an historical resurrection? The answer, of course, is that the data consist in the collective experience of the Church, as expressed in the Bible, the Creed, and other writings and teachings. The data are comprised by the whole body of material that has come together in what we call doctrine, *dogma* – the teaching of the Church.

E.   DATA AND FACTS IN THEOLOGY;
TRUTH CLAIMS ONCE AGAIN

Conventional religious wisdom (which includes opinion that is highly sophisticated in areas other than religion) may find this just too much to swallow. Surely, this is nothing other than a great *petitio principii*. We have tried to identify the unique contributions that theology has to make to our understanding of religion and the religious, over and above what psychology and sociology have to offer, and we seem to have ended by saying that theology has such contributions to make, providing we are willing to accept without question the dogma, the creeds, the Bible – all those things that theology was supposed to have helped us to understand. Have we not merely assumed that which was to have been explained?

The objection misses its target, because it confuses the methods and objectives of apologetics and dogmatics. The central issue is, what constitutes the *data* for each? We recall from our last chapter that data and facts are different things: not all data are facts – and not all facts are data. For the apologetic theologian, the data must indeed be facts. For the method of correlation, those data are the existential, phenomenological facts of human suffering, joy, fear, love, guilt, anxiety, and so on. Insofar as those are imbued with the sense of ultimacy.

The data of the dogmatic theologian, on the other hand, are the dogmas, the doctrines, the affirmations of faith, the *credo*. Strictly speaking, by the principle enunciated in Chapter III, we need not concern ourselves with the truth status of these doctrines, since their truth or falsity does not affect their ability to function as data. But, of course, neither we nor the theologian can be satisfied with this state of affairs. A realist understanding of theology presses us to ask for the reality that lies behind Church doctrine. To be sure, Church dogmas are real things; but the reality of the dogmas (e.g., the creeds) will not satisfy the demands of realism. Words are not the same as the things to which the words refer, even if both are real. It is for the latter that we seek, not just the former.

Professor Torrance responds to this by claiming that behind the dogmas is the Dogma, behind the data, the Datum (pp. 343 ff.). The dogmas, e.g., the creeds, constitute the data for the theologian (for which reason Barth called his major work *Kirchliche Dogmatik – Church* Dogmatics). But *behind* the data lies the Datum, the Datum of Revelation, the fact of God in Jesus Christ.

To call the Datum of Revelation a "fact", as Professor Torrance does, suggests very strongly that it is *part of* the theologian's data. Indeed, Professor Torrance reinforces this by saying such things as that theological statements "refer to an objective reality above and beyond them, and . . . are true in terms of that reference" (p. 173). It is not that theological statements are designed or intended or thought to refer to such an objective reality (by which we can assume he means the Datum of Revelation), but that they do in fact so refer and are true precisely because they so refer.

It is absolutely crucial to our understanding of theology that we see that such a view is wrong. The Fact of God in Christ is never one of the facts with which the theologian deals; the Datum of Revelation is never part of the theologian's data; the Dogma is never an element of the dogma. The affirmation of the Fact, the Dogma, the Datum of the Revelation of God in Jesus Christ is an article of *faith*. What makes a person a Christian, and what makes a theologian a Christian theologian, is that he affirms this. It is therefore a pre-condition or pre-supposition of the whole enterprise of *Christian* theology; it is not part of that enterprise. Dogmatic theology proceeds on the basis of the data, which are constituted by the dogmas. Those data are not revealed by God to the theologian; rather he discovers them in the teachings of Bible, Church and Creed, and his discovery of them is a purely empirical process, just like the entomologist's discovery of his data about the boll-weevil.

This important fact about theology helps to blunt a criticism that is often made of dogmatics, namely, that it is dogmatic. Dogmatics is often regarded as if it, the theology itself, were revealed. Unfortunately, Professor Torrance's statements lend some credence to such a view. But, of course, theology is not revealed. Professor Torrance's theology is a product of Professor Torrance's mind; it was not revealed to him by God. Professor Torrance, like all other Christians, believes that God is definitively revealed in the person of Jesus, by virtue of which we call him the Christ. That belief, incorporated into Church doctrine, becomes part of the data for the theologian. But God did not produce the theology; God produced or begat – so Christians believe – Jesus.

I am not saying that Professor Torrance himself subscribes to the view that in dogmatics the theology itself is revealed. He is careful to point out, for example, that "as a *science* theology is only a human endeavor in quest of the truth . . . It takes place only within the environment of the special sciences and only within the bounds of human learning and reasoning" (p. 282). Nevertheless it is clear that Professor Torrance believes that theology occupies a privileged position among the sciences by virtue of having available to it a body of knowledge, the Datum of Revelation, that is not available to other sciences. It is this belief that I am here concerned to dispute.

The activities of the theologian are as fallible, and his theories as corrigible, as those of any other scientist and any other theories. The dogmatic theologian is no more dogmatic than a physicist or a mathematician. "Dogmatic" refers to the data, not to the mind-set, of the theologian. Indeed, the parallel between dogmatics and natural science is very close indeed. The "dogmatic inversion" does not mean that the theologian is entitled to spin out his theories from some set of postulates taken by the theologian as either arbitrary assumptions or as self-evident truths. Quite the contrary, as Professor Torrance puts it, dogmatics involves "the kind of knowledge that is forced upon us when we are true to the facts we are up against" (p. 341). But I want to make it quite clear that in my view, which may not agree with Professor Torrance's, the facts to which dogmatics refers, the data of dogmatic theology, consist entirely in Church doctrine.

In emphasizing the differences in data and method between dogmatics and apologetics, I may have left the impression that there is a kind of opposition between the two kinds of theology. This cannot be the case. Since both are Christian, they must both function within the context of the Christian point of view as set forth in Bible, Creed and Church. The dogmatic theologian is not empowered to legislate for our religious experience; but neither is the apologetic theologian entitled to set aside Christian doctrine in the light of some "higher" philosophical or religious truth. Indeed, Tillich once reported a remark of Karl Barth's to the effect that he and Tillich start at opposite ends and meet in the middle. But of course they must insofar as they are both Christian.

The distinction in method between dogmatics and apologetics suggests the distinction between formal and factual science, or between the formal and factual aspects of science. We can say that in apologetics the "existential correlates" in the method of correlation correspond to the observational side of scientific theory. The observational vocabulary is in experiential terms (suffering, joy, guilt, love, anxiety, etc.), where those terms refer to experiences that are so deep, so profound, so moving as to warrant our calling them "religious". On the other hand, dogmatics corresponds to the formal structure of scientific theory. Here, the data are not experiential, but occur in the doctrines of Bible, Creed, and Church, and the vocabulary of dogmatics consists of a set of theoretical terms drawn from those doctrines.

This being the case, we may fruitfully apply the metatheoretical criteria developed in Chapter III to theology in order to refine our concept of what constitutes the discipline of theology, and to spell out in detail the isomorphism between science and theology. That is the task of the following chapter.

CHAPTER V

Metatheology and Metascience

This indirect comparison of theological science with the other sciences requires to be undertaken in our day, not for apologetic purposes or for the achievement of some kind of scientific security for theology within the same terms as the other sciences, for that could never be valid, but for quite a different reason, in the interest of theological purity and in the struggle to prevent theology from degenerating into an ideology. (Torrance, 1969, p. 285)

Theology must indeed be prevented from becoming ideology: a mere system of what William James called "brain-born ideas". But, for reasons that will become evident later on, we must be very careful about the notion of purity in theology as in science. What Professor Torrance means by purity is something like self-contained-ness, and the implication of this is that we are interested, theologically, only in the consistency of the system of ideas in its attempt to represent its object, viz., the Datum of Revelation. I believe that we are interested in things other than this and, at the same time, I have already given reasons for being cautious about the role of the Datum of Revelation in theology. We will consider some further reasons for caution shortly.

In any event, purity cannot be equated with security, and if purity as an ideal for theology be rejected, it does not follow that we have given up security as well. Indeed, it is the essential purpose of this chapter to argue that theology can in fact achieve scientific security. This is not a mere matter of redefining theology in such a way that it can ride around on the coat-tails of physics and mathematics; this is why I have tried to look at dogmatics and apologetics as they are practised and not as I think they should be practised. What I believe is that theology – that is, dogmatics and apologetics – is entitled to be regarded as science in its own right.

As noted in Chapter II, we must be careful not to erect criteria for "science" in such a way as to exclude from the club all applicants except physics and mathematics. In particular, the Received View, which we have taken as a model metatheory, is just that – a *model* – and a model is not a literal description. The application of the metatheoretical criteria, especially the formal ones, must be tempered to the degree of formalization of the special science in question. Our metatheoretical considerations may apply to economics and sociology with more reservations and qualifications than to physics and mathematics but that does not mean that we can, by metatheoretical fiat, rule that economics and sociology are not sciences. The same will be true of theology.

A. THEOLOGY'S CLAIM TO "PRIVILEGED STATUS"

But Professor Torrance says that this can never be valid, and his reason is that in theology, unlike any other science, we apprehend or recognize "divine realities" (loc. cit.). I disagree with this, and in order to justify the opposite conclusion – that theology stands on its own merits as a science among other sciences – I will make an effort to apply to theology the metatheoretical criteria developed in Chapter II to see if they mark out a scientific theological discipline commensurable with the other special sciences. If the metascientific criteria of Chapter II also serve as metatheological criteria, then we will have reason also to believe that we have fairly arrived at a general meta*theory*, such that we no longer need to distinguish between meta-*science* and meta-*theology*.

If we are successful in arguing that theology is a special science, or very much like one, there will be a price to be paid, and that price will be the "purity" of theology. But then, as Bunge has pointed out, science is not very pure either. Despite efforts to formalize scientific theory, it is rarely possible to do so, even in mathematics, and so science falls back on "reason" or "rationality" in a broader and looser sense. Sacrificing purity in science, however, may have an enriching effect by virtue of encouraging, or at least permitting, cross-fertilization among the sciences, and even by the absorption into the sciences of the intuitively rational common-sense perception of the world.

What theology sacrifices is its claim to stand alone among the sciences by virtue of its access to "divine realities" denied to all other forms of intellectual activity. So be it. In the first place, I believe that such a claim on behalf of theology is spurious and will so argue later on. Moreover, it is precisely the claim to privileged status that has won theology so many enemies – even among the faithful. For many Christians see this as a claim on the part of the theologian to know something that the ordinary Christian does not. In one respect, the claim is true, the sense, namely, in which the psychologist has a more systematic knowledge of my anxiety than I do, knows more about its cause and effects, and perhaps knows what to do about it. But if there is any privileged knowledge about my anxiety, it is I that have it, not the psychologist. My physician may be able to do something about my headache, but it is *my* headache and I have a knowledge of it that no amount of medical learning can duplicate or reproduce.

Similarly, the "plain man" may be nowhere near as expert in the analysis and manipulation of religious concepts as the theologian, but he is vastly closer to, "tuned into", what those concepts are concepts of, than is the theologian *qua* theologian. The great temptation of theology is to suppose that *real* knowledge of the religious dimension depends on one's theological sophistication; from there it is only a step to the belief that one can be a *real* Christian only if theologically and hence intellectually sophisticated. The conveying of such impressions has not won theology a great deal of popular support, even among those allegedly served by theology.

Thus, if we forfeit the purity to which Professor Torrance attaches so much importance – the status of theology as a system closed to everything except the "divine realities" to which it alone has access – if these are forfeit, I say, it may be the case that theology wins a wider respect than it has so far, and also by humbling itself to the status of the other sciences, theology may be instructed as to what it can and cannot profitably do.

I have been maintaining a distinction between dogmatic and apologetic theology. But this distinction must be taken with a grain of salt: it is misleading to treat them as if they were quite distinct, not to say opposed, enterprises. More about this will be said in the next few pages. Moreover, I would not want to suggest that the dogmatic theologian is insensitive to apologetics or *vice versa,* and there are always elements of both in each. Still, I will continue to treat them as disparate until later in this chapter when there will be reason for talking about *theology* without the adjectives "dogmatic" or "apologetic". This will be a consequence of the application of the rubrics of metatheory which will be seen to require both dogmatics and apologetics, thus supporting the view that there is really only one intellectual enterprise called theology with its dogmatic and apologetic aspects, rather like experimentalism and theory in physics.

First, however, let us recall what I have called the constitutive criteria for scientific theory and see whether the Received View comes close to characterizing theology. The simplified version of the Received View held that a fully formalized theory is (1) axiomatized; (2) has a vocabulary consisting of *(a)* logical terms, *(b)* theoretical or technical terms, and *(c)* observational terms; and (3) supplies a set of correspondence rules relating the theoretical and the observational terms. These characteristics were enunciated with a fully formalized theory in mind. However, as we saw in Chapter II, even when allowance was made for the non-formalization of most scientific theories, the constitutive characteristics above were found applicable in an easily recognizable form. Are they applicable to theology?

B. AXIOMATICS AND DOGMATICS

I am contending that dogmatics is the formal part or dimension of theology. The content of dogmatics is supplied by dogmas, doctrines, creeds, scripture, the teachings of theologians, commentators, etc. This material consists of a set of primitive terms that are undefined (and undefinable) within dogmatics, and a body of propositions that are unprovable within the theology.

It is perhaps not too far-fetched to think of the Creed as such an axiom set. Words like *God, Son, Christ, begotten, ascended, sins, holy,* and *world-to-come* would all be primitive terms. Similarly, the propositions of the Creed, to which speakers of the Creed profess their assent, would be the axioms: that God is the maker of heaven and earth, that Jesus Christ is begotten of God before the world, that there is a life of the world to come, etc.

Now, of course, it might be argued that the Creed is not primitive-independent or postulate-independent, but that within the Creed some terms are definable by other terms (e.g., that *Christ* means *Son of God*) or that some assertions of the Creed are really theorems in that they can be deduced from other propositions of the Creed (e.g., that "God created heaven and earth" is deducible from "He created all things visible or invisible", since everything in heaven and earth is either visible or invisible). Were this to be the case, it would merely show that a dogmatics based solely on the Creed was a non-independent formal theory.

More likely, however, it would be maintained that the Creed does not stand alone, and that in order to understand the terms and propositions of the Creed, reference must be made to, say, the Bible. Or the theologian might draw on other teachings of the Church to give an accounting of, for example, the meaning of "heaven and earth". What is essential, however, is that for the purposes of dogmatics, the sources must be Bible, Church, and Creed. The theologian may not go to Greek philosophy or planetary physics, for then the warranting evidence comes from *outside* the doctrine and we are back in apologetics. This is what Professor Torrance means by the "purity" of theology.

How far the theologian can cast his net for primitive terms and basic postulates is a matter of debate. For example, are the Church fathers legitimate sources of doctrine or not? What seems evident is that the Church is never isolated from the world, and, therefore, philosophical, scientific, and popular ideas impregnate religious concepts. Inevitably, the data of dogmatics are infected with material that is not unique to the tradition that generates the dogmas, material that is, for that matter, not even uniquely religious. For this reason, one should speak with caution about the purity of theology.

However that may be, the effort in dogmatics is to build something approximating an axiomatic system that contains a set of *logical* terms (*one, all, the, is, and, only*) and a number of technical or *theoretical* terms (*God, Christ, Sin, resurrection, redemption*). We need to be careful about the *observational* vocabulary, however. The first, and rather trivial, reason is that some of the referents are not observable at all in any ordinary sense. For example, the Virgin is not on hand to be observed, nor can I "see" the ascension.

The second, and more subtle, difficulty with an observational vocabulary in theology is that those creedal terms that do seem to stand for something observable (*father, virgin, maker, son*) have a way of being transformed, by the dogmatic inversion, into peculiarly theoretical terms, the referents of which are not to be confused

with the referents of the ordinary-language analogs of those terms.
E.g., "maker" in "maker of heaven and earth" is not like "maker"
in "cabinet-maker". This sounds suspiciously like what happens in
scientific theory where, as we saw, each successive candidate for the
observational vocabulary ("black hole", "visible star", "radio
waves") turns out to be yet another theoretical term: the theory
"gobbles up" reality. In consequence, the distinction between
theoretical and observational in theology as in scientific theory, and
the status of the correspondence rules in each, is considerably less
than clear.

This leads one to suspect that dogmatics is really an almost
entirely uninterpreted system, despite the occurrence in it of familiar "religious" language. Indeed, there are metatheories about
theology (e.g., Phillips, 1971) that come very close to saying just
this. However, my own flirtation with formalism has to do only
with the formal side of theology, i.e., with dogmatics. Dogmatic
theology, in my view, does not deal directly with the referents of
religious language (e.g., God, Redeemer, Sin), any more than
Euclidean geometry deals directly with those objects to which the
terms and concepts of geometry may be applied. Dogmatics *is* a
formal system and it is because of this that the metamathematical
criteria can be applied to it, *mutatis mutandis*.

What I object to is a theological short-circuit whereby dogmatics
is presumed to have some direct access to the data, the objects, the
referents of religious language. It is for this reason that I believe that
dogmatic theology must be complemented by apologetic theology.
It is quite true that metatheoretical formalism with respect to
dogmatics would deny any existential relevance to theology were it
not for theology's empirical side, namely, apologetics.

The qualification *"mutatis mutandis"* is important here: it is not
the case that the formalism of dogmatics is just like the formalism
of geometry. And the reason for the difference is that the interpretation of geometry is, by metatheoretical fiat, frozen. New forms of
experience to which Euclidean geometry is inapplicable do not
bring about a modification of Euclidean geometry; rather, we
merely invent a new mathematics, leaving Euclidean geometry just
as it was, applying to just those elements of our experience to which
it previously applied.

Metatheoretical fiat is not, however, a luxury that the theologian
can afford. Dogmas, religious formulae, are crystallized out of
ordinary language under the pressure of religious experience. But

religious experience is only ordinary experience invested with the dimension of depth or ultimacy. As our experience changes, so does the language in which we try to represent that experience. As "time makes ancient good uncouth", so the changes in our experience over time make ancient religious formulae irrelevant. There is, however, of necessity, a fluidity in the dogma that is not paralleled in the language of geometry. As changes in religious language occur, there must be corresponding changes in the formal theory, the theoretical vocabulary of which is constituted by that language, i.e., in dogmatics. Thus it follows that no dogmatic theology can ever be regarded as "final": the work of the dogmatic theologian is never done. This is a point that we will arrive at by a rather different route later in this chapter.

C. FORMAL CRITERIA APPLIED TO DOGMATICS

Thinking of dogmatics as an axiomatized system, let us turn our attention to the *formal* metatheoretic criteria to see if, and in what way, they might reasonably be said to apply to dogmatics.

1. *Consistency.* Wheelwright, in the well known book *The Burning Fountain* (1954, pp. 60 ff.) discusses the contrast between "literal" and "expressive" language, and points out that while such a logical construction as paradox could not be tolerated in literal discourse, it can not only be tolerated, but may be rather uniquely appropriate in expressive uses of language. Shelley is writing a poem about a skylark – a bird. In his first couplet, he says, "Hail to thee, blythe spirit/bird thou never wert". In any literal use of language, this would, of course, be intolerable. The lecturer in biology who began the morning's lecture by saying, "Today we begin our discussion of the skylark, which is not a bird", would be thought quixotic, to say the least. But for Shelley's poetic purposes, such a paradox seems quite appropriate. Wheelwright offers many interesting examples of such usage.

This is not the time to develop a theory of religious language (although I will attempt to outline such a theory in my last chapter). And I am not altogether happy with a view that holds religious language to be "merely" expressive. Such a view has been advanced by R. B. Braithwaite (1955). Nevertheless, it does seem to me that religious language cannot be regarded as literal, or flat-out descriptive. Therefore, the treatment of language in theology can be expected to differ from the treatment of language in scientific theory.

Specifically, the application of a metatheoretical criterion such as consistency needs to be understood in light of the nature of the language of the theory to which the criterion is being applied. Despite the efforts of some philosophers of science (e.g., Hesse, 1966) to argue that science contains irreducibly metaphoric elements in which paradox might find a home, the prevailing view (see Bunge, 1973, pp. 106 ff.) is that paradox in science is intolerable (hence Bunge's efforts to dispose of the complementarity principle in quantum mechanics).

In theology, however, paradox may be not only tolerable but essential: Jesus is wholly God and wholly Man; we are free, but God's omniscience allows him to know in advance what we will do; sin is the state of separation from God, but God could have created us sinless; and the famous trilemma of natural theology – God is good, God is omnipotent, and there is evil. Without entering upon the examination of any of these paradoxes, I want to observe only that our metatheory must not be so restrictive as to rule them out *a priori*.

This means that "consistency" must not be understood in such a strong sense that any statement of the form "p and not-p" is rejected out of hand. What consistency does mean is that the theological structure must hang together, cohere, constitute a whole rather than an *ad hoc* collection of bits and pieces of symbolism unrelated, or only loosely related, to each other – a kind of theological rag-bag. In order to set this metatheological characteristic apart from the strictly logical notion of consistency, I will call this criterion, as applied to theology, *Coherence*. To assert that a dogmatic system is coherent is to assert its *Zusammenhang*, its hanging-together-ness, perhaps even in the face of logical oddities such as paradox.

Even though we take issue with Professor Torrance over the matter of purity in theology, he is surely correct in saying that the subject matter of theology marks it off from the other sciences (just as, of course, it is the subject matter of agronomy that makes it different from apiary science). In particular, the subject matter of theology has to do with the perceived relationship between God and Man, the "intersection" of the divine and the human. Such an intersection may necessitate linguistically odd, and even logically odd, usages such as paradox: Wholly God and wholly Man. This should not be understood to mean that we are given license to babble on in any way that catches our fancy. (Unfortunately, there is a tendency to think of theology in just that way: the stringing together of "religious" words in such a way as to convey the impression of a profundity, which is merely pretentiousness.) Dogmatics must remain faithful to its data, just as astronomy must be faithful to observation. The data of dogmatics are the teachings of the Church (as the body of Christian believers). The religious experience of Christians, embodied in the Christian religion and represented in Church doctrine, is normative for theology; the theologian is no more entitled to cut himself loose from the tradition than is the agronomist to disregard the findings of plant physiologists.

Lest it be supposed that I am playing fast and loose with well-established and clearly delineated metatheoretical criteria, such as consistency, by transmuting it into something else, viz., coherence, and then claiming that the same criterion applies both to science and to theology, let me say a word about a characteristic such as consistency. Why is the mathematician interested in consistency? Why is *anyone* interested in consistency? Surely not because Euclid or Peano or Hilbert or all of them put together decided that it would be nice to have a consistent system. We have already seen that in an *in*consistent system, we can prove anything whatever. Such a system would be packed full of whatever anyone wanted to have in it. In short, were it inconsistent, we would have no *system* at all, but would have a mere collection of whatever appealed to the subjective interest of the collector.

Well, one might say, but what is so bad about that? What is bad is simply that it violates our commitment to a set of ideas that constitutes a whole, a unit, a coherent intellectual structure. It is, I am urging, the intellectual drive toward *coherence* that brings about the elaboration of such a metatheoretical criterion as *consistency*: coherence is prior to consistency. Thus in talking about a metatheological criterion of coherence, I am not merely watering down the good, rigorous metamathematical concept of consistency; I am rather appealing to a concept that is epistemologically prior to, and gives substance to, the more restricted metamathematical idea. The same will turn out to be true of each of the formal criteria.

2. *Independence*. Following the procedure above, I will use the term *Economy* to denote the metatheological analog of the

metamathematical idea of independence. Independence, it will be recalled, means that no primitive term can be defined with reference to the other primitive terms, and that no axiom can be proved as a theorem of the system. What this means for theology is that the fundamental machinery with which the theologian works is kept to a bare minimum. The theologian introduces no more concepts and no more propositions than the dogma requires.

One of the problems that westerners, and in particular western Christians, have with oriental religions is what appears to us to be a plethora of deities. To us, accustomed to at most a trinity, it appears that Hinduism is vastly oversupplied with divine figures. If three persons are adequate to the religious task at hand, why postulate any more? The same consideration applies to the debate over the elevation of the Virgin to the status of co-redemptrix. Christianity seems to have gotten along fine with Father, Son, and Holy Spirit (and sometimes the Protestant may even feel a little uneasy about the third person); why do we need a fourth? Needless to say, Unitarians employ the same argument in the other direction.

To make the virgin a fourth Person and thereby to create a Quaternity in place of the Trinity would appear to turn a theorem into an axiom and a defined term into a primitive, producing a non-independent system. There may, of course, be some other reason for doing this – some reason, perhaps, lying outside the dogmatic system altogether. It might have been mandated by a re-examination of the dogma, the Church doctrines, re-examination having shown that the present Trinity did not adequately account for certain Christian beliefs. That would have to be argued. It should be noted that even if the system so produced was *not* independent, there would have been no logical damage done. What would have been violated is our desire for economy.

As in the case of coherence, economy ought not to be looked on as a pale imitation of the full-blooded metamathematical criterion of independence. It is rather the other way around: independence in an axiom system is a formalization of the prior *desideratum* of economy. The principle of Occam's razor (that we ought not to multiply entities beyond necessity) predates the development of metamathematics by a good many centuries.

3. *Completeness*. In metamathematics, completeness means that every proposition that can be stated in the language of a theory can be proved or disproved, or, alternatively, that every such proposition or its denial is a theorem. The metatheological analog I will call

Adequacy. The question is whether a theology is rich enough to deal adequately with all of its data, i.e., with Church doctrine in its entirety. One difficulty with our regarding the Creed as an axiom system is that in its economy, it is not sufficiently well endowed with concepts and postulates to speak to the full range of religious concerns. If, for example, it is the business of Christianity to address itself to issues of economics, politics, education, or even morality, it is an open question as to whether Christian dogma contains enough material to make that possible. The answer to this question will be found in a critical examination of the doctrines of Bible, Church, and Creed. If the answer is No, then it would appear that the dogma has achieved economy at the expense of adequacy, and that it may be necessary to augment the dogma with material drawn from other appropriate sources.

It is the task of critical metatheory to be clear about such questions. What *are* the primitives (terms and axioms) of dogma? What really *does* the theologian have to work with? What can the theologian *really* conclude? Metatheology must always warn against importing non-dogmatic ideas (from economic liberalism, for example, or political conservatism) and dressing them up in Christian clothing in order to build them into Christian dogma, and from there into theology. It is required that theology look to see what is really there in Church doctrine; that is the force of Professor Torrance's demand that theology proceed in "obedience to the facts". Theology should be adequate to speak to all the relevant concerns as defined by the dogma, *and no more*.

The priority of *adequacy* to the metamathematical concept of completeness follows straightforwardly by analogy to what I have said about economy and coherence, and I will say no more about it.

4. *Interpretation*. As we have seen (Chapter II), from the standpoint of formal axiomatics, it is not crucial what kind of, or even whether, an interpretation can be given, except insofar as the test for consistency involves the giving of an interpretation. However, as in the case of geometry, the utility and the interest of a theology very much depend on our ability to give a successful interpretation.

Were we to carry through the axiomatizing process using the Creed as the axiom set, we would have to replace a word such as "God" with a meaningless symbol like Γ, "Jesus Christ" with Λ, "son of" by σ, etc. so that we are not tempted to import material from the familiar, anthropomorphic meanings of those words. But such "sentences" as $(x)[(x=\Lambda)\equiv x\Gamma\sigma]$ are not likely to arouse much interest, let alone to illuminate our faith. Thus, to make theology relevant to the actual content of religion, in fact, to ascertain *whether* theology is relevant, an interpretation is required. So crucial is this to theology, in contrast with other formalized theories, that it deserves to be considered a criterion in its own right rather than as a mere appendage to the criterion of consistency. I would call this metatheological criterion, this analog to interpretability, *Existential Relevance,* and it represents the demand that theology be actually capable of addressing those articles of faith that constitute the Christian religion.

So much for the *formal* metatheoretical criteria; we now turn to the *empirical* or factual criteria. The criterion of existential relevance (above) has already imposed on theology an empirical or factual dimension, for it is an empirical fact that these are or are not the doctrines of the faith. But note that the requirement of interpretability (existential relevance) still only carries us as far as the dogmas themselves. What is yet needed is to close the gap between dogmatics and religious experience. This cannot, however, be accomplished from the side of dogmatics itself; instead, we begin from the side of religious experience and see whether our existential concerns are addressed by Church doctrine – whether the teachings of the Church in Bible and Creed illuminate and help us to make sense of the facts of anxiety, guilt, etc. But this is precisely what Tillich's method of correlation does, i.e., this is the task of Christian apologetics.

It is in just this sense, namely, in Church doctrine, that apologetics and dogmatics "meet in the middle", as Barth said of his and Tillich's theologies, and that they are not only complementary activities, but require each other for successful completion of the systematic theological mission. We may now speak of apologetics and dogmatics together as systematic theology – or simply, theology.

D. EMPIRICAL CRITERIA

Recall that Bunge's first factual metatheoretical criterion was 1. *external consistency,* i.e., the requirement that the theory be consistent with "the bulk of corroborated data, hypotheses, and theories". This means that theology must "fit" with other theories including, most importantly, scientific theories, insofar as we regard a scientific theory as "corroborated" and insofar as we accept that theory. In the event of contradiction between science and theology, one or the other must be modified. It is a metatheoretic requirement that at the level of theories, contradiction cannot be accepted.

Similarly, whether in science or theology, theories must fit the data. Thus, theology must square with religious experience insofar as that experience is corroborated, e.g., shown not to have been hallucinatory. To an objection that we are selective about which data are regarded as corroborated, we reply that, of course, we are. That is a consequence of data being theory-laden. It is also a consequence of the fact that theological affirmation must square with "the *bulk of* corroborated data, hypotheses, and theories". It is not fair to pick out this or that observation, fact or experience and treat it as definitive. We ruled out the experience of a man who, allegedly under orders from God, murders his child. We ruled it out because it does not fit with the *bulk* of other beliefs that we hold, such as that "God is love", that "He desireth not the death of a sinner", and so on. We would want to know a great deal about the whole life and personality of the child-slayer before we were willing to regard his experience as "valid". That is, our belief in this case must fit the whole range of data from non-religious sources (e.g., psychology) as well as from peculiarly religious sources.

2. *Scrutability*.   The propositions of theology must be testable against the data of religious experience. In the Received View, "testing" means verification or falsification. This issue has received a large amount of attention in recent years, beginning with the falsifiability debate in Flew and MacIntyre (1955). In that debate, however, and in much of the subsequent literature, the question is the falsifiability of *religious* belief, and the argument is whether religious convictions or beliefs are or are not testable against empirical data in the way that scientific beliefs are. Such an argument (whichever side it is on) confuses religion and theology, however. The question is not the verifiability or the falsifiability of *religious* beliefs, but the testing of *theological* propositions.

In the case of theology, the requirement of scrutability seems to require either Tillich's method of correlation or something closely akin to it. We test our theology, our (partially formalized) theory, by seeing whether what we have to say, theologically, about the dogma, about the content of the faith, is correlated with and helps us to make sense of the facts of our religious experience. This process is mediated through the language of Bible, Church, and

Creed. The task of theology is to look "upward" from existential concerns to the doctrines that are presumed to illuminate those concerns (the apologetic side of theology), and also to look "downward" to those same doctrines that constitute the interpretation of the formal system (the dogmatic side). Scrutability thus requires both sides of the theological enterprise.

3. *Explanatory power.* One purpose of scientific theory, perhaps the most important purpose, is to explain things, to help us to understand those things more fully than we did before. It will be recalled (from Chapter II) that one way a theory can explain is to predict, especially in the sense that we would have been able to predict an event had we known the antecedent conditions before the predicted event actually occurred. But as also noted, theories are not mere predicting engines. A fully explanatory theory enables us to predict, but it does more than that: the theory sets the thing to be explained into a context, a pattern, tells a story about it, and our understanding of it consists in our seeing it in its relationship to other elements of the pattern, in its "role" in the story.

We need only observe here that theology provides the pattern within which to set the experiential details of religion. Theology attempts to spell out a *system* in which religious concepts and the experiences to which they refer are assigned their roles or places. By virtue of the double-edged nature of theology, we understand religious concepts in their formal character by the essentially axiomatic nature of dogmatics, and we understand the factual reference by virtue of the existence-correlates of apologetics. A theology has explanatory power if and only if its theoretical vocabulary is hooked into an observational language derived from religious experience.

This condition is not always fulfilled, however. As Tillich noted in *The Dynamics of Faith* (1957, p. 43), symbols grow and die. A particular piece of religious language may have been meaningful at some time in the past, but it now fails to evoke any response. This is the case with the symbol of the Virgin for the Protestant: the symbol no longer has existential relevance. Metatheory would call for the revision of theology's primitives under these circumstances to prune away a technical term that is no longer needed. A theology that is freighted with existentially irrelevant terms and with propositions that bear no relation to our religious experience is like an astronomy that insists on retaining epicycles when they are no longer needed to explain anything.

Theology's explanatory power would seem to be restricted to this sense of setting a context or pattern within which to place our religious concepts. That is to say, it would seem far fetched indeed to claim for theology any predictive capabilities. It is sometimes argued that if one were willing to undergo the discipline of the mystics, then one could also share in the religious experience of the mystics. That is, to be sure, a prediction of an experience that one will have, and the fulfillment or nonfulfillment of that prediction would constitute verification or falsification of the hypothesis. However, that hypothesis does not seem to be peculiarly a part of any *theological* system but is, perhaps, a piece of psychology of religion. In any event, the inability of theology to predict does not damage its claim to provide an explanation of religious phenomena.

E.   PRAGMATIC CRITERIA

With respect to the *pragmatic* criteria, it is necessary to note only that a theology's "utility" (a word that sounds rather forced in this connection) is really identical to its explanatory power. A theology is "useful", religiously speaking, if it explains, helps us to understand, religion and the religious. If it does not help us to understand (and there are many who find some kinds of theology singularly unilluminating), then it is useless – existentially irrelevant.

The aesthetic quality of a theology is the same as the aesthetic quality of any theory: the simplicity, the elegance, the economy of a theory commend that theory to us; the lack of such qualities make the theory seem cluttered and overly ornate. So the western Christian may regard eastern Orthodoxy, and so the Christian may regard Hinduism. Exuberance of symbolism may, of course, reveal a wealth of fascinating detail about the life and thought of the participants in such religions, but from the standpoint of theology, the symbol system seems simply overburdened. For the same reason, the baroque church does not, for most of us, I suppose, have the aesthetic power of the cleaner and more economical gothic style; and the religious significance of the Hindu temple seems to us to get lost in the welter of symbolism.

F.   REVELATION AND THE GÖDEL
INCOMPLETENESS THEOREM

Only one topic remains now to be discussed. It may seem that I have been too willing to dispense with what Professor Torrance calls the Datum of Revelation. I have claimed that the data of the dogmatic theologian are constituted by the doctrines of the Church – the dogmas. And it may seem that in setting aside the Datum from which, in Torrance's view, the data spring, I have tacitly, at any rate, suggested that revelation is irrelevant to the theologian. That is not true, although the way in which revelation enters the picture is not easy to specify. We deal here with the parallel of the distinction in the philosophy of science between the "logic of theory" and the "logic of discovery". The way we handle data, facts, and theories themselves once we have them is, it is maintained, different altogether from the way we discover things, including the way we invent theories. Whether or not the distinction is as sharp as some claim, the fact remains that the distinction must be recognized. Flashes of insight, hunches, intuitions, and wild guesses do not figure in the Received View's picture of scientific theorizing.

And yet, we have seen one or two indications that scientific metatheory must allow for the flash of insight by which theory is augmented, amended, or perhaps even overturned altogether. This is the theme of Thomas S. Kuhn's *Structure of Scientific Revolutions*. Bunge, it will be recalled, was concerned to note the importance of material from outside the formal theory itself, saying that by the importation of such material, "the crust of a formalized theory is pierced" (see above, p. 30).

The situation is similar with theology. The metatheoretic claim that the crust of formal dogmatics is pierced, is to say that there must be a crack through which revelation can make itself felt in theology. To deny this would be tantamount to a decision by the theologian as to what God could and could not do. But how can metatheory handle this problem without simply opening the doors to admit all claims to new truth, no matter how trivial? How can we demand completeness of theories, and at the same time leave open the possibility of new truth?

The answer is that we cannot. Moreover, metatheory has conclusively showed that we cannot. The import of this is extraordinary: until recently, the incompleteness of theories could be regarded as an unfortunate deficiency, to be remedied by further theoretical work. But the Austrian mathematician, Kurt Gödel, demonstrated in the 1930's that any axiomatic, i.e., fully formalized, theory in mathematics that is reasonably rich in primitive terms and axioms (e.g., rich enough to generate arithmetic) is incomplete. This "incompleteness theorem" (the extraordinarily ingenious proof of which we cannot discuss here) means that if the system is consistent, then there are propositions statable in the language of the system such that neither they nor their denials can be proved in the system. This is not because we have not enough time or ability to prove all theorems; rather it is a metamathematical statement about the very nature of axiomatic systems themselves.

Obviously, this theorem does not apply to inconsistent systems, because in such a system, as we have already seen, any proposition whatever can be proved. Thus, the Gödel theorem shows that if a system (such as mathematics) is consistent, it is *necessarily* incomplete; if it is complete it is *necessarily* inconsistent.

This remarkable achievement brought into question many of the deepest convictions of science, mathematics, and philosophy, particularly that the way to Truth was through formal theory. Many philosophers from Plato onward had believed that mathematics was the model for all truly rational thought. But the Gödel results show, not only that it is impossible to build a final and complete body of knowledge, but that it is impossible to prove the consistency of any formal theory that we have developed or that we will ever develop in the future.

The Gödel theorem might be supposed to lend comfort to the enemies of reason, reason having been shown to be forever and necessarily inadequate to achieve full and final knowledge. Bunge, however, draws precisely the opposite conclusion. He says, "Irrationalism should not rejoice in the essential incompleteness of almost every theory: what is incomplete makes further rational investigation possible and desirable" (1972, p. 242).

What Bunge means is that every sufficiently rich, and therefore interesting, theory is "open" in the sense that new axioms can be added to it in order to make it possible to prove those theorems that were previously unprovable. Where do such axioms come from? From the mathematician's ingenuity and imagination, from the physicist's further exploration of the world. Thus, instead of closing off further research, the Gödel theorem constitutes an invitation to further and yet further research. No matter how rich and powerful our theories, they can always be made richer and more powerful. As Bunge says, "there is no end to the task of building stronger and stronger theories" (loc. cit.).

The extension of this to theology, and particularly to the role of revelation should be obvious. Just as theory in mathematics and the natural sciences must be open to new insights and new disclosures about the nature of the world, so must theology be open. No theology can lay claim to final Truth. The religious expression of this is that all theology must always be ready to hear the word of God. It is in this way that the Datum of Revelation enters the theological picture.

It must be carefully noted, however, that such a statement does not imply that it is to the *theologian* that God speaks. The theologian's data are public and available to anyone: namely Church doctrine and the religious experiences that underlie that doctrine. God's self-disclosures will be in and through those experiences, with respect to which the theologian occupies no position of privilege.

Theology is religion's theory and will exhibit the same strengths and limitations as any other theory. In particular, the Gödel results have shown that the price of completeness in axiomatics is inconsistency (only an inconsistent system can be complete). Inconsistency in mathematics is a fundamental and fatal flaw, a kind of original mathematical sin. Similarly, to claim that theology is now final and complete, to close theology to the possibility of revelation, is to assert that God has no further capability for self-disclosure. But to make this claim is to say what God can and cannot do; it is, in effect, to make oneself God, and this is what theology has always known as Sin.

CHAPTER VI

Some Applications

As suggested in the introduction, my essential task is now complete. What I have done is to "try on for size" a view that science and theology are methodologically isomorphic as evidenced by the fact that the same metatheoretical canons apply, *mutatis mutandis,* to both. This calls into question the common view that science and theology are radically different kinds of enterprises, employing vastly different methods, and that they are perhaps even antithetical to each other if not mutually exclusive.

The argument with respect to science and *theology* must not be confused with a similar argument that might be made with respect to the relation between science and *religion.* The early years of this century produced a large number of books designed to show that science and religion are incompatible. More recently, the pendulum seems to have swung the other direction, and we now find authors such as Ian Barbour (1974) arguing that science and religion are not only compatible but share many methodological characteristics.

I have not spoken to this latter issue at all; I will, however, have some things to say about the matter of religious language and religious belief in the next and concluding chapter. For the time being, suffice it to say that I believe that the entire science/religion debate rests on a fundamental mistake. That mistake consists in treating religion as if it were a theory on a par with scientific theory. But as I have argued throughout this book, it is *theology,* not religion, that is to be compared with science. To ask whether science is compatible or in conflict with religion, whether the scientific or the religious account of creation is true, whether the scientific method is to be preferred over the "religious method", is simply to confuse the theoretical levels at which these activities go on.

Even in the case of science and theology, however, I have not really proved anything; specifically, I have not proved that theology is a science to be lined up alongside physics and chemistry and mathematics. If someone has a different account of the nature of theology or of science, then he or she will come to a different conclusion than I do. Such a difference would have to be displayed, and we would have to see whether that conclusion agrees as fully or more fully with what scientists and theologians actually do than does my picture of science and theology.

What I claim is that when we look at theology through the eyes of the Received View, which I have taken as a kind of model metatheory, we find that the criteria by which we judge a theory – constitutive, formal, and empirical – apply to theology in a way that is as illuminative of the theological enterprise as it is of science, and that it yields as accurate an account of theology as it does of non-formalized theories in, say, the social and behavioral sciences.

It is important to note that I have not tried to make theology out to be a science on all fours with the natural sciences by simply *defining* theology in such a way as to make them parallel. Rather, I have tried to represent theology as it is actually done. The fairness of my representation may be supported in a modest way in the next few pages when we come to look at some specific theological positions.

If the parallel between science and theology is as I have represented it, the theologian will approach his data in a way that is comparable to that in science. This is not to say, however, that all theologians approach their data in just the same way, any more than all scientists do so. Specifically, this approach will vary depending on whether the formal or the factual side of theory is emphasized. In some of the sciences, such as biology, the main thrust is factual; in others, such as physics, the emphasis may be on the formal side. Some sciences, such as anthropology, have virtually no formal aspect, while others, such as economics, seem to be moving toward a true and fruitful mix of formal and factual. Theology is also a mix of formal and factual, and while those two sides are jointly required for a full understanding of religion and the religious, their differences must not be overlooked.

This has all been very abstract, and it is legitimate to wonder whether a study of concrete theological views would bear out what has been said about the nature of theology. To respond to this, I propose to look briefly at three concrete examples of the theologian's work. These will be creedal formulas, because, as already seen, it is possible to think of the creed as a kind of formal theory in miniature. The question before us is, given what has been said about the nature of theology and the metatheoretical criteria applying to it, what shall we make of these creedal statements? How does the foregoing discussion shed light on the theologian's treatment of these affirmations of faith?

The three articles with which we will be concerned are "Creator of heaven and earth", "Born of a virgin", and "Ascended into heaven". In the eyes of many, these affirmations are central to the Christian faith, and that is one reason for looking at them in particular. Another reason is that among all the articles of the Christian faith, these three go most strongly against the scientific grain. If, therefore, I can make a case for these being propositions comparable to the constituent statements of a scientific theory, the parallel between science and theology will have been, to that extent, substantiated.

I will look at the way in which each formula is handled by a dogmatic theologian and then by an apologetic theologian. In each case, the former will be Karl Barth, and I will use his small *Dogmatics in Outline* (1949), rather than the massive *Church Dogmatics I.1* (1936). The apologetic treatment will come from Paul Tillich's *Systematic Theology* (1967). In the consideration of each formula, I will introduce the "top down" approach of dogmatics and the "bottom up" approach of apologetics with a "motto" from Barth and Tillich, respectively, but will thenceforth render their views in my own words rather than attempting to select apt quotations for that purpose.

After having looked at these three articles of the Creed in their theological settings, I will conclude with a few metatheological comments on Barth's and Tillich's approaches in order to tie these concrete examples back into the metatheoretical inquiry of the preceding chapter.

A. CREATOR OF HEAVEN AND EARTH

1. Barth:

> "It is impossible to separate the knowledge of God the Creator and of His work from the knowledge of God's dealings with *man*. Only when we keep before us what the triune God has done for us men in Jesus Christ can we realize what is involved in God the Creator and His work." (1949, p. 52)

To confess God the creator, to affirm the belief that God created heaven and earth, is not to make some kind of pseudo- or pre-scientific statement about what is the case with the world and its origin. We are confronted, not with a set of empirical facts, the explanation of which is to be found in the causal agency of some hypothetical entity called "God". The opening article of the Creed does not present us with a scientific puzzle, but with "the mystery of faith".

But what is this mystery? That we do not understand how the world came to be and so we produce a god to explain it? Not at all, for that would merely replace one mystery by another. Moreover, it would be procedurally improper, from a theologian's point of view, because it begins at the wrong end. The standard, scientific, empirical procedure (or so conventional wisdom would have us believe) starts with the facts, *viz.*, the world, and infers to the existence of that which is problematic, *viz.*, God. But the dogmatic inversion turns this the other way around. What is given to us is God, not the world; it is the world that is problematic, not God. What should surprise us is not that there is a creating God, but that there is a world that he created.

What is known is what is given to us in the dogma, in this case, that God created heaven and earth. It is not our theological mission to question that. What we are required to do is to demonstrate how those things that are given dogmatically hang together in a consistent whole. So it is not a matter of *proving* anything; *a fortiori* it is not a matter of proving that God exists or that he creates. The question is, what does God's creating *mean*? Not, surely, that we have an hypothesis as to the origin of the world and all things in it, an hypothesis that we set over against those of astronomy and biology. The *meaning* of God's creation is to be understood in the light of the other affirmations of the faith, namely, "what the triune God has done for us men in Jesus Christ". The world is made, not begotten; Jesus Christ is begotten, not made. But since we deal here with a Christian confession, not with a philosophical or scientific theory of cosmology, our affirmation that God is *creator* must be made in relation to our further affirmation that God is *father*: "I believe in God, the father almighty, maker of heaven and earth". Our Christian knowledge of creation is not read off the empirical surface of things but is dependent on our further knowledge that God the father became man in his son Jesus Christ. Just as we look forward and backward in time from the incarnation, so we look outward to the world from the central fact that in the middle of creation and the creative process is God become man in Jesus Christ.

By creating the world in a free and gracious act, and then by becoming part of that creation, God endows the world with meaning. By virtue of the incarnation, the world becomes a human world. Our actions, particularly our creative actions, are lifted out of their merely causal connections and are endowed with a freedom and purpose that mirrors God's creative freedom and purpose. It is God's action in the world by his son Jesus Christ, his gracious action "for us men and for our salvation", that makes the world meaningful.

"Creator of heaven and earth" cannot, therefore, be understood simply as standing by itself like some kind of hypothesis to be tested against the "facts" and in competition with other, and more properly scientific, theories. The "facts" of the world are what we *see* them *as*, viewed through the eyes of the Christian faith, or of some other faith or theory or blik. For the Christian, the "spectacles behind the eyes" are constituted by the faith confessed in the Creed; God as "creator of heaven and earth" means nothing until set into the whole pattern of Christian belief and related internally to all other articles of the faith.

2. Tillich:

"The doctrine of creation is not the story of an event which took place 'once upon a time'. It is the basic description of the relation between God and the world. It is the correlate to the analysis of man's finitude. It answers the question implied in man's finitude and in finitude generally. In giving this answer, it discovers that the meaning of finitude is creatureliness." (V. I, p. 252)

What is the "question implied in man's finitude"? We organize and structure our world in terms of four categories: time, space, cause, and substance. In each of these categories, our finitude is manifest. I exist only in the present; but the present is forever slipping away and I move inexorably toward my end-time, my death. I exist only insofar as I occupy a space, a place; but I am always threatened with loss of place (home, country, job) so that I am insecure. I exist only insofar as I can control my life; but I seem to be in the grip of forces over which I have no control. I exist only insofar as I have a substantial self, an ego; but when I search for myself I seem to find only images of what I wish I were or how I appear to others.

In each of the categories, I am finite and, being finite, am threatened by the loss of being, by the ultimate victory of non-being. Consequently, I am anxious. This is the constant theme of modern drama and art and philosophy. The loss of a sense of history (time), of community (space), of effective power (cause), of integrity (substance) are the symptoms of modern anxiety. And, above all, we are anxious about death.

These are the facts, the data with which Tillich begins. It is to these facts that Christianity must speak if it is to have what we have called "existential relevance". What does belief in God, "creator of heaven and earth", have to say in response to the existential fact of anxiety. As evident from the above, the question of finitude cannot be answered from within the finite condition, for it is that very condition that poses the question. The answer must come from the other side, from the side of the revealed word of God. This is the method of correlation.

God is creator of heaven and earth. Our finitude is our creatureliness. The religious correlate of finite creatureliness is divine creativity. We are created, we are part of creation, we are a product of the divine creativity. Therefore, we participate in that creativity. Our creatureliness carries with it the threat of non-being – that is what it is to be finite. But we also participate in being-itself, in the "ground of being"; otherwise, we would not be at all. The legacy of non-being is, for us, anxiety; the heritage of being in us is courage – the "courage to be", to affirm our being in the face of the threat of non-being.

Our participation in the divine creativity assures us of our freedom – not in the absolute sense in which God alone is free, but in our creaturely, finite freedom. We are *in* being, and that is the meaning of the doctrine of creation. But we are also *outside of,* or separated from, being – our essential being – and that is the meaning of the doctrine of the fall. Our finite freedom, our creatureliness, resides precisely at the intersection of these two:

precisely insofar as we both participate in and yet are separated
from the ground of our being.

Our finitude, our creatureliness, our anxiety, are not set aside by
the fact of our participation in the ground of our being. But our
faith in God as the ground of being and meaning and as the power
of being, and in God's directing, providential creativity, is the
source and principle of the courage to be with which we meet our
anxiety.

B.   BORN OF A VIRGIN

1. Barth:

"[We have considered the assertion, 'conceived by the Holy Ghost'.] And
now we have to turn the page and come to the second thing . . . when we
say, 'born of the Virgin Mary'. Now the fact is underlined that we are on
earth. There is a human child, the Virgin Mary; and as well as coming from
God, Jesus also comes from this human being. God gives himself an earthly
human origin, that is the meaning of 'born of Mary the Virgin'." (p. 47)

"Conceived by the holy ghost" and "born of the virgin Mary"
are conjoint pronouncements, the meaning of which is that God
freely became a man. It is not that God became *Man* in some
abstract, philosophical sense, but that he became *a man,* this particular man. So the Creed says ". . . was incarnate by the holy ghost of
the virgin Mary *and was made man*".

These are the "axioms of the incarnation", and it should be
recalled that the doctrine of the incarnation is the analog of the
doctrine of creation. Within creation there is another and special
creation – the *unio hypostatica* – the once-and-for-all union of God
and man in this man. But the Creed also instructs us that Jesus
Christ is "begotten of his father *before all worlds*". The Christian
message has three parts: (1) in our time an event occurred, Jesus
Christ was born of the virgin Mary; (2) this event was not an
historical accident, but was willed by God from eternity, "before all
worlds"; and (3) that all of this is not a mere pyrotechnic display of
God's creating virtuosity, but is "for us men and for our salvation".
That is what the incarnation is about.

But why do we need two articles: "born of a virgin" and "made
man"? The former is the miracle of Christmas, the latter the
mystery of the incarnation. The incarnation is the thing itself – God
made man; the virgin birth is the sign of that thing. In the
Christmas story, we deal not with conception-in-general and

birth-in-general, of which Jesus' conception and birth are but
particular instantiations. Rather, we deal here with a very definite, a
very unusual conception and a very definite and unusual birth. The
miracle of Christmas is the miracle of *this* conception and *this* birth.

But is it *true*? The Christmas story is not the invention of the
theologian; it is the confession of the Church. The theologian's job
is not to try to get behind that confession in order to determine
whether it is true or false, but to make sense of it. Suffice it to say
that if someone wishes to argue that the story is *false,* he must do so,
not on some neutral, theory-less basis, but on the basis of *his*
theology. Where, in Christian belief, the incarnation has been
accepted and understood in the light of all the other affirmations of
faith, that is, where we acknowledge the central mystery of the faith
("and was made man"), and where no attempt has been made to
reduce the faith to something it is not, e.g., science or philosophy,
then the miracle of Christmas can be "thankfully and joyously
recognized" (p. 100).

2. Tillich:

> "Jesus, like every man, is finite freedom. Without that, he would not be
> equal with mankind and would not be the Christ. God alone is above
> freedom and destiny. In him alone the tensions of this and all other
> polarities are eternally conquered; in Jesus they are actual. The term
> 'sinlessness' is a rationalization of the biblical picture of him who has
> conquered the forces of existential estrangement within existence. As early
> as the New Testament, such rationalizations appear in several places, as, for
> example, in some miracle stories – the story of the empty tomb, the virgin
> birth, the bodily ascendance, etc." (V. II, p. 127).

Barth is right in connecting the doctrine of incarnation with that
of creation. If, however, we reject a literalistic account of creation, it
will be also necessary to reject a literalistic understanding of the
pre-historic paradise of Eden. Following this out, the fall will turn
out to be, not an historic event, but a symbolic representation of the
transition from a state of "dreaming innocence" to a condition of
full self-awareness. God did not create a state of affairs that was
good (i.e., the Garden) which was later transmuted into something
bad by the intrusion of an alien, evil force. The story of the fall is
the symbolic story of man's coming to his real, his existential,
condition – the condition of self-awareness and self-affirmation.
This condition is one of estrangement from God, from other
beings, and from himself.

But what could all this have to do with the virgin birth? A
non-literalist account of Genesis compels us to the view that

creation and fall are inter-woven, that "actualized creation and estranged existence are identical" (V. II, p. 44). To put it still another way, sin, i.e., estrangement from God, is the very nature of man's existence. But in the incarnation, God has transcended our old, sinful state and has established the New Being in which estrangement is overcome. The bearer of that New Being is Jesus, and for that reason we call him the Christ.

The biblical picture of Jesus contains representations or "rationalizations" of his status as bearer of the New Being, as the one in whom esistential estrangement has been overcome – paradoxically – within existence. One of these representations is the story of the virgin birth. What is the point of the story? – that Jesus is thoroughly finite, like us, that he is subject to all the temptations of finitude as we are, and that he has overcome these temptations (personal, economic, political) in order to maintain the relationship with the Father without which he would no longer have been the Christ.

But is it true? The miracle stories, including the story of the virgin birth, are religious statements. To ask if they are true, as we would ask of a statement in biology, is to try to transform an "existential-symbolic" statement into a "rational-objective" proposition (V. II, p. 127) and thereby to misunderstand the story.

The point of the story of the virgin birth is the incarnation. The virgin birth is represented as an event in time and space; the incarnation is timeless and placeless ("before all worlds"). Both are necessary: the incarnation, because the reconciliation between God and his creatures is eternally true; the virgin birth, because that eternal act must, if it is to be of relevance to us, be manifest in a finite being, a person. Beyond this, "no inquiry is possible and meaningful" (V. II, p. 127).

C.   ASCENDED INTO HEAVEN

1. Barth:

"The Ascension does not mean that Christ has passed over into that other realm of the creaturely world, into the realm of what is inconceivable to us. 'On the right hand of God' means not only the transition from the conceivable to the inconceivable in the created world. Jesus is removed in the direction of *divine* space, which is utterly concealed from man. It is not heaven that is his abode; He is with God." (p. 125)

The resurrection is not a "spiritual" event: there was an execution, there was an empty tomb, then there was a visible presence after death. The promise has been fulfilled, the victory has been won. Note the past tense. To be sure, the combatants are still making their moves as if the outcome were in doubt, but that is only the vestigial remnant of the old; the new has already come into existence.

What is the meaning of the ascension? It is that Jesus, the resurrected Lord, has left our space, earthly space. But he has not gone to some never-never land: he is with God in God's space, *divine* space. We may call that space "heaven", provided that we understand the word to mean, not some other part of the created world, but the world, the space, of God the creator. The creator's world is not, of course, some world that is spatially different from our world; the creator's world includes and completes and fulfills our world as (we might say) the mind of the poet includes and completes and fulfills the poems that he writes. Jesus' ascension thus completes and fulfills his mission with us. As God was humiliated and suffered in the person of Jesus on the cross, so we are carried up and exalted with Jesus in his "mighty resurrection and glorious ascension". With Jesus, we are "seated on the right hand of the Father".

With the ascension, we begin a new time, the time of the Church – "One, Holy, Catholic, and Apostolic" – in which we confess our belief in the third article of the Creed. It is the time in which, in faith, we wait for the denouement, the climax of the whole drama in which Jesus, the Christ, "shall come again with glory".

Thus we look backward and forward from the ascension: that act completes the first part of the drama of God's relation to man, and it directs our attention toward the second part and, ultimately, toward the great and final in-gathering of creation – the "life of the world to come".

2. Tillich:

> "We must now consider a consistent group of symbols, taken from the rich field of eschatological symbolism, which corroborate the Resurrection from the point of view of its consequences for the Christian, his Church, and his world. These start with the symbol of the Ascension of the Christ."
> (V. II, p. 161)

Biblical symbols do not occur in isolated, unrelated bits of imagery, but are clustered around the central themes of the Christian story. One such cluster centers on and "corroborates" the resurrection. This cluster includes the story of the virgin birth, the feeding and healing stories, and the ascension. Therefore, the previous formula, "born of a virgin", and the present one, "ascended into heaven", are not two unrelated stories, but are each pointed toward the (historically) intervening event of the resurrection.

As in the case of the virgin birth, we can ask why there are *two* symbols – resurrection and ascension – and not just the story of the resurrection. The answer is that the ascension carries with it a sense of finality, of closure. The resurrection story is followed by repeated experiences of the risen Lord; after the ascension, Jesus is separated from historical existence.

What is symbolized by the ascension? If it is a story corroborating the symbol of the resurrection, we may approach an understanding of the ascension by inquiring after the point of the resurrection story itself. This is not merely another of the familiar legends of gods and demi-gods who died and came back to life. There is no religious, which is to say existential, significance to a story about an individual who was dead and then later was not dead. This would be a remarkable story, but utterly devoid of religious interest. What makes the resurrection/ascension story religiously significant is that these things happened to this same man who is the subject of the incarnation/virgin-birth story. The whole point of the incarnation/resurrection (and so of the virgin-birth/ascension) story is the appearance of God-manhood (V. II, p. 150), that is, the New Being, the Christ, under the existential conditions of estrangement. "Came down from heaven" and "ascended into heaven" are spatial metaphors, and we should not allow ourselves to be led off the point by pictures of Jesus rising up through the clouds. The point is that after the crucifixion Jesus' followers had an extraordinary and transforming experience which led them to connect the concrete figure of Jesus with the reality of the New Being: they *saw* Jesus *as* the Christ. Moreover, we confess Jesus to be the Christ because we, like the disciples, like Paul, like "many", experience the living presence of the New Being. Where healing, feeding and comforting take place, where people are made whole, there is the New Being. The event – for us as for the disciples – did not occur 2000 years ago, but occurs here and now, wherever and whenever estrangement and alienation are overcome. It is the reality of this experience that we clothe in the symbols of resurrection and ascension.

D. COMMENTS

The foregoing has not, of course, constituted anything like an explication of the positions of Barth and Tillich with respect to the three doctrines of the Church. But, in their rudiments, I believe that my summary has been faithful both to the spirit and the content of those theologians' views. What I have tried to do is not only to convey spirit and content, but also to capture the tone and flavor of their styles. Those theological styles are vastly different, and it would be a serious mistake to underplay that difference. And yet we may have come away with the feeling that Barth and Tillich are not so far apart as their contrasting styles would have initially led us to expect. This is surely what Barth had in mind when he said that he and Tillich meet in the middle. What ties them together, of course, is the fact that whether they come from the top down or from the bottom up, they must meet in the Christian message, the *kerygma,* for they are both Christian. For both, the articles of faith are given; no theology, whether dogmatic or apologetic, has legislative power over the content of the faith.

Barth seems more "literalistic", while Tillich is inclined to think and talk in terms of symbols. But Barth is no fundamentalist; nor is Tillich an existential philosopher. Barth will simply not respond to the question, "But is it *true?*" That is not his business. If I have questions about verifiability or falsifiability, that is *my* problem and not Barth's. His task is to "unpack" the dogma, not to make judgements of truth or falsity about the dogma, in just the same way that it is the geometer's task to explicate that which is contained in the axioms, not, *qua* geometer, to ask whether those axioms are true.

In an interesting way, Tillich is not concerned with truth either, if by "truth" we mean verifiability, as in the Received View. Tillich's interest is in the way in which the doctrines of the faith, symbolic though they may be, help to make sense of our experience. Not those experiences with which scientific theory deals, but with those existentially urgent experiences of anxiety, fear, loneliness, etc.

Barth's attention is focused on the *internal* meaning of the dogma, as the formalist in scientific theory is concerned with internal consistency among, and deducibility from, the postulates of the formal system. Tillich, on the other hand, focuses on the *external* relevance of the dogma, in a way parallel to that in which factual or empirical theory in science is concerned with the mapping of the formal theory onto the external world. I must hasten to add, however, that the existential relevance of doctrine is as important to Barth as is internal consistency to Tillich. It is a question of the difference in theoretical focus, not of indifference to the legitimate concerns of the other. Were that not so, there could be no meeting in the middle.

It is my hope that even in my abbreviated capsules of the dogmatic and apologetic approaches to questions of doctrine, even in the fragments lifted out of the contexts in which alone they can be fully understood, it will still be seen that, and in what way, dogmatic theology and apologetic theology bring light to our understanding of religion and the religious. When Barth finishes his explication of a creedal formula, when he has exhibited the way in which that formula fits into the wider pattern of creed and scripture, we are enlightened: we grasp the particular more firmly now that we understand its role in the larger pattern, just as we understand a particular assertion in science when we have seen how it fits into the total pattern that constitutes the theory. And when Tillich has pointed out to us the relationship of this creedal formula to other aspects of human thought – science, myth, philosophy – and has exhibited the way in which this article of faith correlates with our own existential concerns, we are again enlightened: we "get the point", just as we get the point of a scientific proposition when we have been shown that and how it fits with "the bulk of corroborated data, hypotheses, and theories", as Bunge says – when its external consistency has been demonstrated.

The final and important thing to see here is that Barth and Tillich, dogmatics and apologetics, are not two antithetical ways of doing theological business, any more than theoretical and experimental physics are somehow opposed or are pulling in opposite directions. Both are required for a full account of the phenomena under consideration. As Hanson reminds us, it is not only prediction (as in experimental physics), not only axiomatizing (as in theoretical physics) that produces a satisfying explanation, but both together. Similarly, it is neither dogmatics nor apologetics that accomplishes the theological task: each is complementary to the other.

The three formulas I have discussed are among those that pose the greatest difficulties for serious rapprochement between persons of a scientific, and those of a more religious, temper. And yet, when we read Barth and Tillich, we may come away feeling that railing against these religious expressions in the name of science misses the fundamental point. As noted earlier, theology and science each has its own domain; neither is entitled to set itself up as an arbiter of experience or discourse in the domain of the other. The geologist, *qua* geologist, has nothing of interest to say about the religious affirmation that God created heaven and earth; the theologian, *qua* theologian, has nothing to contribute to an evaluation of the fossil record. This is the lesson we must learn before we can even hope to resolve the unfortunate dispute over "evolutionism" *vs.* "creationism" in the American public school science curriculum. In the next, and concluding, chapter I will raise some questions of a *philosophical* nature about the meaning and truth of such religious assertions as we have considered from a theological point of view in this chapter. It is important that we keep the two kinds of question separated. Theology cannot give us a philosophical or scientific warrant for the truth of an affirmation of faith; science and philosophy cannot afford a vantage point from which to see the religious significance of such affirmations. What Barth and Tillich have done is to give us a theoretical framework within which to understand these doctrinal statements in their religious meaning, insofar as we are disposed *ab initio* to grant the possibility of religious significance to anything at all. Whether we are so disposed depends on the spectacles behind our eyes: what there is to be seen depends on the presuppositions we bring to the seeing. This is why Tillich said that beyond the experience of the disciples by virtue of which they called Jesus the Christ, no inquiry is possible or meaningful.

CHAPTER VII

Meaning and Truth

Throughout the preceding chapters I have determinedly kept my focus on *theology* and have avoided questions about the content and reference of *religious* assertions. The reason for this is that my task has been to explore the relations between science and theology. There is a widely accepted view that it is the relation between *science* and *religion* that should command our attention, rather than the more recondite question of *science* and *theology*. Underlying this entire essay is a conviction that this view rests on a fundamental mistake; a confusion of type levels. The object of theological study is religion and the religious experience; the object of scientific study is the world disclosed to us in and by our ordinary experience. Theology and science are, therefore, first-level theories: our experiences are what those theories are about. Accordingly, the study of the relation between science and religion involves an illegitimate crossover of type levels: it is a study of the relation between two things that are not related. Such a "study" can only lead to confusion.

In this concluding chapter, I take leave of metatheory in order to examine some issues involving religious beliefs and the language in which those beliefs are expressed. However, a *caveat* is necessary, lest it be supposed that I intend to argue that God really did (or did not) create the world or that Jesus was (or was not) in fact born of a virgin. I have no special source of information on those matters, and my opinions carry no greater weight than the opinions of my readers. Instead, my concern will be with the *questions* of meaning and truth, not with the answers to those questions. Thus, this last chapter will be a *theoretical* discussion, in contrast with the *metatheoretical* investigations of the preceding chapters. However, the theory involved in this chapter will be *philosophical* rather than *theological*.

There are several reasons for undertaking this inquiry into the meaning and truth of religious utterances. First, it will seem to many readers (as, indeed, it seems to me) that after our long and rather formal discussion of theology, we ought to pay some attention to that which theology is about, namely, religion and the religious. Religion is the *raison d'être* of theology, and it would seem odd to close this essay without so much as a word about religion itself.

Second, the previous chapter (on "Applications") has already raised the question of truth; not truth in theology, but truth in religion. To affirm our belief in the articles of the Creed and in the content of the Bible – creation, virgin birth, ascension – without at some point asking the question, "But are these things *true*?" would be utterly strange. As we have seen, both Barth and Tillich sidestep this question – quite properly, from a theological point of view. But it is not necessary for me to be so restricted in my inquiry.

Finally, our metatheoretical inquiry has been undertaken only because we are interested in theology. But theology would be a completely pointless enterprise were it not for the fact that we are religiously concerned. A theologian who had no particular interest in religion would be like a film critic who did not enjoy going to the movies. But we are religiously concerned; otherwise, I presume we would not be writing or reading this book. Therefore, it is appropriate that I conclude with some discussion of the meaning of religious belief and religious language, and with some observations about the truth status of those beliefs and of the propositions in which those beliefs are expressed.

A. IS "GOD-TALK" MEANINGFUL?

What is the problem? Put simply and concisely, when we assert that "God created heaven and earth" are we speaking meaningfully or not? And if we are, what is the meaning of the assertion? Moreover, if "God created heaven and earth" is meaningful, is it true? And if it is, how would we find out? We must not lose sight of the context of this inquiry: we are not asking questions about meaning and truth as we would ask them about propositions of a scientific theory or about theological assertions. "God created heaven and earth" is not a pre- or pseudo-scientific hypothesis about the origin of the universe. We are not called upon to decide among three "theories": big-bang, steady-state, and God's-creation. Big-bang and steady-state are theories; God's-creation is not a theory at all but a religious affirmation. Our problem now is not with theories and their constituent propositions, but with the characteristics of religious beliefs and religious language – "God-talk".

(1) *Literalism* There are clean and easy solutions to this problem and there are messy and difficult solutions. Unfortunately, the clean and easy ones are not very satisfactory. There are two basic types of clean and easy solutions to the question of meaning and truth. The first is literalism: the Bible means just what it says, no more, no less. When it is claimed in Genesis that God made the world in six days, it means that God made the world in six days. That may be difficult to reconcile with other things that literalists feel inclined to believe, such as stories told by geologists and astronomers, but that is a problem with which the literalist simply has to wrestle. The story about Jesus being born to Mary who was a virgin may pose difficulties because of our knowledge of the biology of higher organisms, but there is nothing about religion, on the literalist view, that guarantees against this kind of conflict.

But a problem of a different sort emerges when we consider a proposition such as "The trees of the field shall clap their hands". This assertion does not conflict with some theoretical proposition in agronomy. The problem is not that Isaiah gives us one account, while agronomy gives a conflicting account of the circumstances under which trees clap their hands. The problem is that trees have no hands to clap, so that no theory whatever can account for hand-clapping on the part of trees.

Nor is the problem one of the integrity of the prophet. If we thought he had been a liar or was demented, we would simply dismiss such nonsense as that the trees clap their hands. It is precisely *because* of the integrity of Isaiah that this is a problem.

Of course, the solution is at hand, and no intelligent literalist is bothered for a moment by this. It requires only that we distinguish between poetry and literal assertions in order to avoid the problem. But can this distinction be made simply on the basis of an examination of the text? Where does poetry stop and literal description begin? If "the trees of the field shall clap their hands" is poetry, why not "born of the virgin Mary", or "creator of heaven and earth"? Clearly, one must have a *theory* about religious language that sorts out what is literal from what is poetic. This means, however, that the Bible is *not* simply accepted at face value as literalism seemed to say at the outset. Rather, our reading of the Bible is, in Hanson's phrase, theory-laden. It is not the Bible alone that speaks to us, but the Bible read through the spectacles of a theory of religious language.

(2) *Non-cognitivism*   Literalism, therefore, fails to solve the problem. The second clean and easy solution is non-cognitivism. We have encountered one version of this in logical positivism, with its view that religious utterances are non-sense, inasmuch as they are neither verifiable nor falsifiable empirically. It will be recalled, however, that that position later modified its stance to allow other, non-literal kinds of meaning to propositions in normative ethics, religion, poetry, etc. Thus, poetry may serve to *express* feelings about something, religious utterances may *evoke* certain emotional states, and moral injunctions may *elicit* desired behavior patterns. In none of these, however, is the transfer of information or knowledge about anything being effected or even attempted. Inasmuch as cognition (*co-gnoscere*) has to do with the state or process or conditions of knowing, Received View philosophers came to call such linguistic usages "non-cognitive".

Non-cognitivism in the philosophy of religion took many forms. It would not be profitable to try to summarize all of them. Among them, one influential view, enunciated by a very distinguished Received View philosopher, R. B. Braithwaite, in an article entitled "An Empiricist's View of the Nature of Religious Belief" (1955), may serve as a non-cognitivist model. What does it mean, Braithwaite asks, to say that "God is love"? Braithwaite takes this Johannine formula to "epitomize the assertions of the Christian religion" (a very dubious assumption, of course, but that is not our question). What happens when a person says "God is love" is not that he conveys some information about God, not that he evidences some knowledge about divine attributes, not that he intends to instruct his hearers about God, but that he is declaring his intention "to follow an agapeistic way of life".

There are (at least) two kinds of declarations. One is a declaration that such-and-such is the case: I declare *that* I am carrying no alcohol or firearms. But I may also declare an intention *to do* something or to behave in certain ways: " 'Do you swear to tell the truth?' 'I do'." I am not making a statement of fact which may be shown later to have been false. We do not punish a person for perjury on grounds that he made a mistake in fact when he "predicted" that he would tell the truth. "I do" signifies an intention, and when I subsequently lie, I have gone back on my word, broken a promise; I have not merely given evidence that my earlier assertion, "I do", was in error.

On Braithwaite's view, religious utterances are of the "I do" sort; they are, paradigmatically, expressions of intentions, not statements conveying knowledge. It is important to see the difficulties attendant upon this view. First, while this analysis may sound fairly persuasive as applied to sentences such as "God is love", it becomes less and less convincing as we move through other statements characteristic of the Christian point of view. Does "He is risen!" signify our intent to live risenly? Does "crucified, dead, and buried" mean that we intend to live buriedly? Such "analyses" are obviously absurd.

Second the purpose of any analysis is to *analyse* what is happening, not to dissolve it. This is the same condition we found in both science and theology. Science may not be able to give us the taste of the soup, as Einstein remarked, but it may not, for that reason, tell us that the soup has no taste. Braithwaite's analysis simply does not take adequate account of what actually goes on in religious discourse. I may, indeed, intend to live lovingly, "agapeistically", and I presume that St John did also. But it is far from clear that that is what St John *thought* he was expressing when he wrote "God is love", and it is certainly not what 2000 years of Christendom has meant when it repeated those words.

Of course, it may be that for 2000 years, Christians, including some fairly intelligent and reflective ones, have all and every one been muddle-headed, and that Braithwaite has finally got things clear, but I doubt it. This is not a mere *ad hominem*: what is required of the philosopher of religion is not that he decide for us on some *a priori* basis what we do and do not do when we speak religiously, but that he *listen* to religious discourse – all of it, not just those parts that fit his "analysis" – and try to make sense of it, just as it is the task of the scientist to make sense of our ordinary experience of the world, and of the theologian to make sense of our religious experience. The philosopher is no more entitled to legislate meaning and truth than the scientist is to create a world by theoretical fiat or the theologian a religious dimension to life. But Braithwaite's "analysis" constitutes just such legislative fiat.

(3) *A Cognitive Approach*   Suppose that we turn things around and begin, *contra* Braithwaite, with the assumption that religious language is cognitive and see where this assumption leads us – we will, again, try it on for size. What might it mean to say that some proposition P is cognitive? To say that P is cognitive is to say that on the "transmitting" side, it is the intention of the speaker (S) to express or record or convey knowledge about something or other. That is, P is capable of being judged true or false, and if P is true, then knowledge has been expressed or recorded or conveyed ("sent out"), whether or not anyone else hears or reads or believes P. On the "receiving" side, we say that P is cognitive if the hearer (H) believes that it is S's intention to express or record or convey knowledge, whether or not that was S's intention.

So when I say "God is love", I am entitled to claim that it is a cognitive utterance because I am intending to convey knowledge about God, even if you think it is gibberish. Again, when you read "God is love" you are entitled to regard that as cognitive even though in fact the sentence is constructed by a machine programmed to select randomly from a dictionary of nouns, verbs, and adjectives.

This is not a theory of language. All I am interested in is an analysis of the situation where a person reads a book (say, the Bible), recites a formula prepared by the Council of Nicaea, or listens to the preacher, and believes that what is being said is designed to express or convey knowledge about something (God, the world, himself). I want to avoid such questions as whether the preacher is really programmed by his seminary training to mouth certain utterances as a conditioned response to the ringing of the sanctus bell, or whether the Bible was really written by a group of Roman charlatans.

I am, therefore, interested in what I take to be the typical case of religious language, namely, the case in which S and H agree that there is a transaction between them being effected by way of a verbal medium, and that the product of that transaction on H's side is a cognitive or "noetic" state which might be ostensively defined as a state of believing, knowing, doubting, affirming, denying, etc.

To say that P is non-cognitive is simply to negate the above. Either S or H believes that the intent of P is *not* to produce or express a noetic state, but is rather to express an emotion, evince or evoke an attitude, give voice to an enthusiasm, etc. The psychological state at issue in a non-cognitive transaction is not noetic, but is affective or conative. Note that in a typical case of religious language, "cognitive" designates a triadic relation among S, H, and P, but I do not exclude the possibility that "cognitive" may also be used to refer to the diadic relations, S and P, or P and H.

B. COGNITIVE, BUT NON-DESCRIPTIVE

I want now to introduce another pair of terms with which to talk about religious language: descriptive and non-descriptive. I will define "descriptive" in a way parallel to "cognitive": a proposition P is descriptive if it is intended by S to describe a state of affairs in the world, or if H believes that P is so intended by S. "Non-descriptive" will be defined in a way parallel to "non-cognitive". The fact that description is theory-laden does not pose a problem for us, but it may pose a problem for S and H if they hold to different theories or bliks.

It is a characteristic of the Received View to link these two very closely: descriptive with cognitive, non-descriptive with non-cognitive. The reason for this is to be found in another philosophical theory called logical atomism, out of which the Received View emerged. This theory holds that our language is decomposable into "atomic propositions" ("x is red"), that the world is decomposable into "atomic facts", that an atomic proposition is true if and only if it corresponds to or mirrors an atomic fact, that molecular propositions are built up out of atomic propositions, and that, therefore, molecular propositions are true if and only if they are constructed out of true atomic propositions. A proposition, in general, is a linguistic entity that states (or corresponds to) a fact or some collocation of facts. Strings of symbols that do not so correspond (e.g., "God is love") are pseudo-propositions and are without meaning. Thus, to be cognitive (or cognitively meaningful), a proposition must be descriptive.

It is my intent to call into question this identification of cognitive with descriptive, non-cognitive with non-descriptive, and to suggest an alternative. Consider the following "square of opposition":

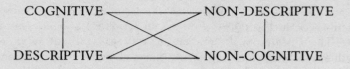

The terms at opposite ends of the diagonals are, of course, contradictories: cognitive/non-cognitive, descriptive/non-descriptive. According to the Received View, the vertical pairs are equivalences: cognitive≡descriptive, non-cognitive≡non-descriptive. If this were true, it would follow that the horizontal pairs are also contradictories: a proposition cannot be both cognitive and non-descriptive or both descriptive and non-cognitive.

It does seem that no proposition can be both descriptive and non-cognitive, looked at from the same side of the communicative process. That is, it makes no sense to say that the speaker intends by his utterance to describe a state of affairs in the world, but intends thereby to express or record or convey no knowledge whatever about the world. Therefore, the Received View seems obviously correct in denying that the bottom horizontal pair can be jointly characteristic of any proposition.

But it is by no means clear that we cannot identify utterances that are both cognitive and non-descriptive, and this is the alternative I wish to consider. If there are propositions characterized jointly by the top horizontal pair, then the Received View analysis of "cognitive≡descriptive" must be given up. The possibility I am suggesting is that there are propositions that are intended to convey knowledge about the world but that are not intended to describe the world. Moreover, these propositions are such that if certain conditions are met, they do in fact convey knowledge about the world and can, accordingly, be called "true" in some legitimate, if perhaps non-standard, sense of "true".

Perhaps an example would help to clarify what I mean by these categories. Suppose I am asked my opinion of the playing of a particular string quartet on a particular occasion. I might respond in several different ways:

(a) Their playing was not quite in tune.
(b) They had a brittle sound.
(c) Phew!
(d) I did not enjoy their playing.

From any of the first three (a-c), one might *infer* that I did not enjoy their playing, but only (d) *states* that fact. Propositions (a) and *(d)* are clearly both cognitive and descriptive; but note that *(a)* describes the quartet's playing while *(d)* describes my psychological state. The third response *(c)* is interesting because it does not state anything, but expresses my negative attitude toward the quartet's playing. It is, therefore, a paradigmatic form of non-cognitive utterance.

The most interesting proposition, for our purposes, is *(b)*. Unlike *(c)*, proposition *(b)* seems designed to convey some information about something. Unlike *(d)*, the information or knowledge that I intend to convey by uttering *(b)* is not about my own psychological state, but about the playing of the quartet, as is the case with *(a)*. But does *(b)*, like *(a)*, *describe* the quartet's playing? The words "in tune" are words that are peculiarly affiliated with music; "brittle", on the other hand, is peculiarly a word that is used in connection with the properties of certain kinds of solids such as Christmas tree ornaments and peanut candy. We would certainly feel hard-pressed to say that the playing of the quartet was literally brittle, in the way that a piece of glass is literally brittle. In fact, in all likelihood, when I utter proposition *(b)*, I have searched around for an adjective that does *not* literally describe (as would "in tune", "off key", "flat", "too slow", etc.) but conveys something of the *feel* of the playing. The same would be true of the application of the words "in tune" to a non-musical situation: "I am not in tune with the Christmas season". I am suggesting that we have here a locution that is intended to convey knowledge about the quartet's playing but is not intended to describe it; *(b)* is cognitive but non-descriptive.

It might be objected that since *(b)* is designed to convey something of the *feel* of the playing, it is not conveying knowledge about the playing but, if it conveys knowledge about anything, the knowledge that it conveys is about my *feelings*. That is, it might be objected, *(b)* is really a close cousin of *(d)* but it is not related at all to *(a)*. But this objection misses the mark. It could hardly be said that it is my *feeling* that is brittle or that I am feeling brittle when I listen to the quartet. It is the playing of the quartet that is brittle, and we ought not to be misled by the word "feels" in the preceding paragraph. The fact that peanut candy feels sticky to me does not, of course, means that I am sticky or that I am having sticky feelings. It is the candy that is sticky. The only force that this objection would have lies in its being pushed to its farthest extremity, where we would say that every adjective used to convey knowledge about something is in reality a description (or characterization) of my own psychological state. But that lands us back in idealism which we gave up several chapters ago.

If this objection fails, I believe I am justified in maintaining that sentences like *(b)* are cognitive and yet non-descriptive. Are such sentences linguistic sports? The Received View thought so, and maintained that our language needed to be precised in such a way as to get rid of these kinds of anomalies. On the other hand, I am proposing that *(b)*-like utterances constitute a very large and very important part of our language which includes metaphors (such as "brittle sound", "splitting headache", "grinding poverty"), but which also includes simile, allegory, poetry, drama, myth – and religious language.

To explicate this fully would require an entire philosophy of language; I can only offer a few suggestions here and recommend that we "try on for size" this proto-theory as it bears on religious language. It should be noted, first, that this kind of utterance is not translatable or explicable without loss into language that is descriptive. The meaning of "grinding poverty" is not the same as an economist's statements about dollar income as compared to national norms. Nor can we merely replace "grinding" by its lexicographic definition: "crush, pulverize, or powder by friction". Obviously grinding poverty is not poverty that crushes, pulverizes, or powders by friction. "All the world's a stage" cannot be reduced to statements about the transitoriness of life, the fact that our actions are in part determined by agents other than ourselves, etc. The proof that this is not possible is that if it were, we could replace *As You Like it,* indeed, we could replace all of Shakespeare and the whole of literature, with a set of scientific treatises. But that is absurd. Its absurdity is most sharply manifest in humor: a joke depends on the fact that it is not translatable; "explaining" a joke leaves no joke at all (see Stenson, 1969).

The reason that this is absurd is that, second, the knowledge gained by such utterances as *(b)* is of a different sort than the knowledge we get from descriptive propositions. "A brittle sound", "grinding poverty", "All the world's a stage", "Hail to thee, blythe spirit!" represent a shift from an external, spectator point of view to an internal, participant point of view. "Grinding poverty" conveys something of the feel of what it is like to be poor; "All the world's a stage" invites me to "try it on", to feel the sham, the pretense, the transitoriness of it all.

Characteristically, the language of science is, or tries to be, "objective". The scientific observer tries to remain "outside" the situation he or she is studying. The psychologist studying anxiety ought not to become anxious; the sociologist ought not to hate the haters whose hate he is studying. Anxiety about and hate toward the objects of scientific study are not calculated to produce very significant pieces of research. So the scientist remains, or tries to become, the spectator. (Contrary to "brute empiricism", the capability and techniques for objective, scientific observation are not presupposed by, but are rather the product of, developed science.)

On the other hand, the theatre-goer who tries to be the mere spectator, who just "observes" the action on the stage, will never understand Shakespeare. Literary criticism is intrinsically interesting, and it may even be of help in taking the "internal" point of view ("Oh yes, now I see what that line means!"), but it cannot be substituted for an engagement with the piece of literature itself. The "lover" who recites passages from Smithers' *Psychology of Love and Marriage* to his beloved merely makes a fool of himself. In each case, confusion arises by virtue of an attempt to substitute the point of view of the spectator for that of the participant.

C. KNOWLEDGE AND THE PARTICIPANT POINT OF VIEW

Of course, it is possible to deny that the internal or participant's point of view carries with it any real knowledge, that the only real knowledge is that embodied in the objective, scientific, external point of view. Essentially, that is what logical positivism said. But that is a mere dogma, a mere denial of the prototheory I am offering, and cannot, therefore, be used as an argument against it. For my part, I am not really attempting to present arguments in support of my prototheory; I am, once again, only recommending that it be tried on for size. If it does not fit (i.e., if it does not fit our experience) so much the worse for it. But it cannot be dismissed on the grounds that it conflicts with a different theory.

In considering the relation between the participant's and the spectator's point of view, it may be of relevance to ask whether the latter (the external point of view) does not actually presuppose the former (the participant's). It seems clear that the only reason we are even so much as interested in an external, spectator, "scientific" point of view is that we are first engaged or involved with the object of that scientific inquiry-to-be. If no one ever fell in love, there would be no occasion for a psychological study of love and marriage. If no one were ever moved to tears by the plight of Romeo and Juliet, it would hardly be worth anyone's time to do a literary study of the play. More damagingly, if poverty were to be understood in merely theoretical terms, the grindingness of poverty would drop out of consideration; and if in our economics and politics, we lose sight of the bad feel of poverty, it will not be long before we lose interest in poverty altogether.

The next thing is to ask ourselves whether these considerations do not also apply to religious language. I must at once enter a *caveat* from a few paragraphs earlier: if someone holds a *theory* about religious language according to which all religious utterances are of the external, spectator variety, their meaning given by the external reality which they purport to describe, then that someone and I will simply be in disagreement. But that other theory cannot be advanced as an *argument* against the view here being suggested: that will merely beg the question.

The prototheory I am proposing is rejected by critics of both the left and the right. The reason is interesting; both conservatism in religion and positivism in philosophy are literalistic, i.e., they both hold that religious language is (or is intended to be) descriptive. Thus, for both fundamentalism and positivism, science and religion are (or may be) in conflict. When they conflict, fundamentalism solves the problem by rejecting science in favor of religion; positivism rejects religion in favor of science. But both come from exactly the same starting point. The view I am advancing avoids both attacks by *(a)* maintaining that science and religion are not in competition at all since they are at different theoretical levels, and *(b)* insisting that in order to be cognitive, religious language does not need to be descriptive, i.e., literal.

At the same time, a non-literalistic theory of religious language must not be allowed to degenerate into a view in which religious language is a mere collection of poetic images, beautiful perhaps, or terrifying, but having no significant relation to the real world. If religious language is to be cognitive, it must convey knowledge about that world and not merely express an attitude toward it. It should go without saying that not all of the language of the Bible, for example, requires such an interpretation. It is quite possible to discriminate among the various kinds of linguistic usages – declarative, imperative, performatory, expressive, etc. – that appear in the Bible and to apply the relevant use criteria.

D.   APPLICATIONS TO RELIGIOUS LANGUAGE

Suppose we now look at one or two examples of religious language to see how this categorization – cognitive and non-descriptive – might work out. Tillich (in the previous chapter) has already set the tone for this. We are trying on the view that the biblical account of creation, for example, is not in competition with Big Bang or Steady State, i.e., does not attempt to give a literal description of the origin of the world, but yet conveys knowledge about the world. What "knowledge" does it convey? The obvious message of the doctrine of creation is that the world has something to do with God's activity; that the world is, indeed, God's handi-work; and that, therefore, we and all other creatures are beholden to God for our existence, our natures, and our relationships. "It is He that hath made us and not we ourselves."

Less obvious, however, is the implication of the doctrine of creation for the point of view or perspective from which we assess our place in God's creation. It is one thing to think of oneself as an autonomous being in a self-ordered world, responsible to no one except insofar as he or she chooses to create (and, of course, dissolve) relations of responsibility. It is quite another thing to look at the world from the point of view of a participant in a cosmic drama that has meaning and purpose, whose relationships are not created by each actor himself or herself, and who is therefore responsible to the Author for the way things go. That is clearly the message of the creation stories in Genesis. In case we should miss that point, the authors of Genesis reinforce it with the story of Adam and Eve naming the animals, an indication of our having been assigned by the Creator a participatory role in his creation: we share in God's creative activity, and we are responsible to God for that which we create (or destroy!).

It is not my point here that the creation stories of Genesis are true, or better than, or to be preferred over any alternatives. I am merely calling attention to the epistemological difference between the spectator's knowledge of the world as embodied in the astronomical/geological/biological account, and the participant's knowledge as represented in the biblical creation stories.

What might we say, from this point of view, about the story of the Virgin Birth? This story illustrates a fundamental characteristic of religious language and, incidentally, of other kinds of cognitive/non-descriptive discourse such as myth and drama, namely, its *holistic* character. Religious utterances do not come in bits and pieces but instead find their proper *religious* setting in the whole story. For the Christian, the whole story, the story of God's relation to the world, is the story of creation, fall, exile, prophecy, annunciation, birth, baptism, ministry, miracles, crucifixion, resurrection, ascension, and second coming. The meaning of Christianity is given in and by that whole story. Moreover, it is the whole story that confers meaning on each episode and not the other way around.

The very word "story" suggests the analogy with drama, and the analogy is quite appropriate since, indeed, God's relation to the world is a drama in which we men and women – along with all other creatures – are the characters. It is not that we are actors playing the parts of the characters – we *are* the characters. It is one of the significant features of drama that separate lines or speeches do not have *dramatic* meaning outside the context of the whole play. Antigone's great speech about the higher law that commands her to bury her brother's body against Creon's decree may be read by itself for its philosophical or aesthetic content, but its dramatic impact is lost without the context of the play as a whole.

But, looked at from the other side, the point of the play could not be made without the particular characters and events that make it up. Change the characters and the events and you have a different play with a different meaning. But what *is* the meaning of the *Antigone*? We might say that it is the conflict between human law and the higher law and the tragedy that results when people like Antigone and her uncle Creon are caught in the middle of that conflict. But why not just say that (or something like it), give a description of the conflict, perhaps an example or two, and then dispense with the play? What does Sophocles have to contribute to our understanding of the conflict that goes beyond what the social psychologist might say?

The answer, of course, lies in the peculiar ability of drama to pull us into the action; we become participants *in* it and not mere spectators *of* it. We are "absorbed" in the play, we "lose ourselves" in it, we literally become unconscious of our existence as separate from that which is being acted on the stage. From this transformed perspective we see the point of the play from the inside and not merely from the outside as spectators. The social psychologist may tell us about role conflicts and we may understand such conflicts as social-psychological phenomena, but when we agonize with Creon over the kingly necessity to maintain civil order in the face of his familial inclinations, our own conflicting desires and duties are illuminated in all their existential poignancy. There is created a consciousness and an understanding of our own situation and that of others that could never have been created by the external point of view of the social psychologist. It is not that the latter is inadequate; it is just different.

Were this not so, then all of literature could simply be replaced without loss by scientific monographs on this or that aspect of morality and culture. While, for most people, this would seem absurd, it may not seem absurd to say the same of religious stories. It may, indeed, seem quite reasonable to propose that we replace all religious language with studies in psychology, sociology, biology, anthropology, etc. Whatever is left over that cannot be said by the sociologist and the biologist, this proposal might add, is simply poetry: aesthetically pleasing, but of no significance so far as our knowledge of the world is concerned.

If a person really believes that "All the world's a stage" is simply false because we can find no footlights or curtains, then it is unlikely that we will be able to persuade such a person that the story of the virgin birth is anything more than a poetic fiction. But if we are disposed to believe that *Macbeth* and the *Antigone* have meaning – existential significance – that transcends this positivistic account, and that particular actions, scenes, speeches, and words in those plays are freighted with meaning and are capable of illuminating our own experience in and of the world, then we may also be disposed to search for the meaning of such scenes and speeches in the Christian story and for the illumination that they can shed on our experience.

Such is the case with the story of the virgin birth. To excise this scene from the rest of the Christian story and to ask for its meaning and truth in isolation from all other scenes that make up the story is to commit exactly the same error as Braithwaite in his decision that "God is love" constitutes the essence of Christianity. "God is love" no more stands alone than does the story of the virgin birth. As Tillich has said (see Ch. VI), the story of the virgin birth corroborates the symbol of the resurrection. Virgin birth and its "parent" symbol of the incarnation are tied to the story of the ascension and its "parent" symbol of the resurrection. But these are inextricably interwoven with the scene of the slaughter of the innocents and its "parent" symbol of the crucifixion. And all of these together are related to the story of the fall – of the Old Adam – and the presentiment of the New Adam, the New Being.

The meaning of the story of the virgin birth, therefore, has to do with God-man-hood: the central theme of the whole Christian story. The story of the virgin birth is not merely a set of propositions asserting the occurrence of some remarkable biological phenomenon. It is a dramatic episode in which we are invited to come with the shepherds to the stable to witness this wonderful event. Whether we accept that invitation, whether we are caught up in the mystery of this particular birth, is parallel to the question whether we can see in Creon our own internal struggles and are illumined thereby. If not, then neither Creon nor the virgin birth, neither the *Antigone* nor the Christian story, is likely to have much meaning for us beyond their mere aesthetic surface.

I am calling attention to the *parallel* between the Christian story and the story of Antigone. This is not, however, to say that religion and drama are the same kinds of thing. In considering the question of meaning, as well as the question of truth (below), our concern is with the nature of the *language* of religion, and not with the substantive question of what the language expresses. Of course, engaging in an act of worship is not the same thing as going to the theater. What distinguishes the language of religion from the language of drama is that the former is employed in the service of those concerns that we regard as ultimate, whereas the language of drama typically is not (although it might be noted that Greek drama had its origin in religious celebration).

E.   THE QUESTION OF TRUTH

Given this contextual and existential understanding of the meaning of religious beliefs and utterances, what can be said about their *truth*? Let us return to the analogy with drama, for if we can say, in some acceptable sense, that the *Antigone* is "true", then it may not sound strange to say that in that same sense, the Christian story is true. Obviously, the problem could be solved by merely stipulating some sense of "true" that will produce the desired conclusion. But I have tried to talk about meaning in a way that does in fact represent what actually happens in the transaction between Sophocles and his audience, between the biblical writers and the faithful, a transaction that produces, or is at least intended to produce, cognition. So now I want to try to keep to a sense of "true" that is not merely stipulated or "fixed up" in order to make the argument come out right, but that is faithful to ordinary uses of that term.

But I have just now exemplified that sense: we are looking for a sense of the word "true" that is *faithful to* ordinary usage. I might have said, a sense of the word that is *true to* ordinary usage, and that is precisely the desired sense. The *Antigone* is "true to" life. Not "true" in the restrictive and specialized sense of empirically verified, but "true *to*": true in the sense that something "rings true", that "her love is true".

Etymologically, "true" has to do with that which is firm, solid, trustworthy. To verify is to make true. From this, we might conclude that the positivistic sense of true is derivative from this more general sense in which I wish to say that the *Antigone* is true. That does not seem far-fetched. What we want in both science and drama – and, we might now add, in religion – is that our utterances be true to the experiences which those utterances are designed to represent, so that the theory, the perspective, the point of view that those utterances set forth do indeed explain, describe, account for our experiences. From an external, spectator point of view, the decision whether theories do in fact explain will be (at least in part) an empirical one. When we deal with non-descriptive discourse, however, as in literature and religion, empirical verification seems inappropriate, or the processes of verification must be broadened out to the point where the term "empirical verification" might better be dropped altogether.

I have said that it is the function of drama and religion to provide insight into our existential situation, to enable us to "make sense of" this or that aspect of self and world, and, particularly in the case of religion and the great myths, to afford a perspective from which to make sense of the whole world and ourselves in it: to comprehend, to grasp-together, the total experience that constitutes our lives. We might then say that religion and the religious story is "true" if it fulfills this function – if it does in fact afford a satisfactory, a satisfying, perspective from which to see the world.

From such a perspective I am able to make judgements about my life and my activities, I am provided with models or standards with which to measure my thought and conduct, I understand events in the world in terms of their interrelationships in a larger and more comprehensive network or pattern. Such are the characteristics of cognitive activity in general, with the essential qualification that in religion our concern is directed toward those experiences to which we attach a sense of ultimacy by virtue of which we call those experiences religious.

Now, if, indeed, religion does in fact enable us to grasp together, to com-prehend, the world, is it extravagant to say that it is, for that reason, *true*? This seems quite close to the point that William James advanced in "Pragmatism's Conception of Truth". In the case of a genuine option between alternative beliefs, James argued, we are entitled to affirm as true the belief that is most satisfying to us, provided that the decision between alternatives cannot be made on grounds either of internal consistency or empirical fact. My only reservation would be that we not regard this criterion of truth as some kind of poor relative of the others. We are entitled to judge that a set of religious beliefs is true, in a perfectly full-blooded sense of "true", if those beliefs hold together consistently and if they enable us to make sense of our lives and our world.

F.   THE PROBLEM OF RELATIVISM, AGAIN

It will, of course, be pointed out that such a notion of truth is "subjective" and "relative", that what satisfies one person may not satisfy another. So be it. We must keep in mind that religion is not some kind of science – proto-, pre-, or pseudo-. We are not trying to apply to religion the metatheoretical canons that are applicable to scientific theory and to theology. All we want to say is that religious affirmations are cognitively meaningful, and that there is a non-extravagant sense in which we can say that they are true.

To be sure, the way I see the world will differ from the way the Eskimo sees the world. The language in which he expresses his *Weltanschauung* will differ from that in which I express mine. His language, insofar as it is religious, will be meaningful in exactly the same sense as mine is. But I do not speak his language, nor do I look at the world through the spectacles behind his eyes. In that sense, as in the case of our ordinary experience of the world of space and time and snow and duckrabbits, our knowledge is blik-laden and therefore relative and subjective.

It must not be supposed, however, that this implies that we are all trapped inside our world views and that nothing can be done toward resolving disagreement. Suppose I say, "It's an elm", and you say "No, it's a hackberry". "Surely not; come over here where I am and look again closely." "Ah, but note the fenniculation of the starple." We try to resolve disagreements about our ordinary experience in these ways: we try different perspectives, call attention to unnoticed aspects, stress this feature and emphasize that, and so on. There is no guarantee, of course, that this process will end in agreement. I may finally say, "Well, I understand all you say, but it still appears to me to be an elm". Lest we find this troublesome, we should note that scientific theory is full of as yet unresolved disputes, some of which may be, in fact, irresolvable.

Now, suppose a Marxist asks why I am a Christian, for he does not understand how that is possible for an intelligent person. Would I not go through something very much like the same procedure as in the hackberry/elm debate? "Just try looking at the world this way." "Doesn't sin seem real? – no matter how hard we try we don't seem to be getting anywhere." "But God *does* love me: so I can accept myself and get on with living even though I know how imperfect I am." Just as in the elm-tree dispute, I invite my Marxist friend to try on my spectacles, I note some aspects of life that he may have overlooked, and I highlight certain features of the Christian point of view that might appeal to him.

If, after having done all I can think of along those lines, my friend says, "No, I'm sorry, I just don't see it", our conversation is finished. But so would be the discussion about the elm-tree. At some point, the evidence presented either seems persuasive or it doesn't, and if it doesn't, the debate ends (although other kinds of persuasion may still be attempted). The mere fact that we cannot guarantee agreement does not, however, cast doubt upon either the cognitive meaningfulness of the propositions in which the debate is conducted, or on the applicability of the notion of truth to those propositions.

In religious terms, this is the problem of conversion, and the process of conversion ought not to be confused with that of proving something to someone. It is safe to say that no one was ever converted to or from Christianity on the basis of, for example, proofs or disproofs of the existence of God. But to suppose that there is only one "rational" kind of approach to verification, *viz.,* deduction or induction, is to lay down a dogma which, because it *is* a dogma, we are not required to accept. That dogma confuses internal with external, participant with spectator, and denies what all of us know to be a perfectly acceptable way of resolving disputes. There is nothing irrational about the patterns of argument suggested above. And if, having run through those patterns, we find that the belief that it is an elm harmonizes with all our other beliefs, or that the belief that Jesus Christ is lord and savior makes sense of an otherwise disharmonious life, it is only philosophical pedantry that denies to those beliefs the adjective "true" because the demands of some *other* theory of truth have not been met.

REFERENCES

Achinstein, P. (1971) *Law and Explanation,* Oxford Univ. Press.

Barbour, I. (1974) *Myths, Models and Paradigms,* Harper and Row, New York.

Barth, K. (1936) *Church Dogmatics I.1,* T. and T. Clark, Edinburgh.

Barth, K. and Brunner, E. (1946) *Natural Theology,* Geoffrey Bles, London.

Barth, K. (1949) *Dogmatics in Outline,* SCM Press, London.

Braithwaite, R. B. (1955) *An Empiricist's View of the Nature of Religious Belief,* Cambridge Univ. Press.

Bultmann, R. (1964) *Kerygma and Myth* (2nd ed.), SPCK, London.

Bunge, M. (1972) "Metatheory", in *Scientific Thought,* UNESCO Div. of Philosophy, Mouton/UNESCO, Paris.

Bunge, M. (1973) *Philosophy of Physics,* Reidel Publ. Co., Dordrecht, Holland.

Carpenter, E. (1973) *Eskimo Realities,* Holt, Rinehart and Winston, New York.

Flew, A. and MacIntyre, A. (eds.) (1955) *New Essays in Philosophical Theology,* SCM Press, London.

Hanson, N. R. (1969) *Perception and Discovery,* Freeman, Cooper and Co., San Francisco.

Hanson, N. R. (1971) *Observation and Explanation,* Harper and Row, New York.

Heisenberg, W. (1958) *Physics and Philosophy,* Harper and Bros., New York.

Hempel, C. G. and Oppenheim, P. (1953) "The Logic of Explanation" reprinted in Feigl, H. and Brodbeck, M. (eds.) *Readings in the Philosophy of Science,* Appleton-Century-Crofts, New York, pp. 319-352.

Hesse, M. (1966) *Models and Analogies in Science,* Notre Dame Univ. Press, Notre Dame, Indiana.

James, W. (1902) *Varieties of Religious Experience,* Longmans, Green & Co., London.

Maslow, A. (1976) *Religion, Values and Peak Experiences,* Penguin Books, New York.

Phillips, D. Z. (1971) *Faith and Philosophical Enquiry,* Schocken Books, New York.

Piaget, J. (1971) *Biology and Knowledge* (trans. Walsh, B.), Univ. of Chicago Press; reprinted in part in Gruber, H. and Voneche, J. (eds.) *The Essential Piaget,* Basic Books, New York, pp. 848-849.

Putnam, H. (1962) *"What Theories are Not",* in Nagel, E., Suppes, P., and Tarski, A. *Logic, Methodology and Philosophy of Science,* Stanford Univ. Press, Palo Alto, California.

Rudner, R. (1966) *Philosophy of Social Science,* Prentice Hall, Englewood Cliffs, New Jersey.

Stenson, S. (1969) *Sense and Nonsense in Religion,* Abingdon Press, Nashville, Tennessee.

Suppe, F. (1977) *The Structure of Scientific Theories,* Univ. of Illinois Press, Urbana.

Tillich, P. (1957) *Dynamics of Faith,* Harper and Bros., New York.

Tillich, P. (1967) *Systematic Theology* (three volumes in one), Univ. of Chicago Press.

Torrance, T. F. (1969) *Theological Science,* Oxford Univ. Press.

Wheelwright, P. (1954) *The Burning Fountain,* Indiana Univ. Press, Bloomington.

125

INDEX OF PERSONS

Achinstein, P., 36

Barbour, I., 89
Barth, K., ix, 62, 64, 69, 91ff
Braithwaite, R. B., 77, 106ff, 117
Brunner, H. E., 62
Bultmann, R., 10
Bunge, M., 29–33, 72, 78, 82

Carpenter, E., 12

Flew, A. G. N., and MacIntyre, A.,
  12, 32, 83

Gödel, K., 86ff

Hanson, N. R., 11ff, 35, 51, 53, 101
Hare, R. M., 12
Hegel, G. W. F., 64
Heisenberg, W., 1, 7, 19
Hempel, C., 32
Hesse, M., 78
Hume, D., 62

James, W., 20, 36, 41, 43, 48, 71

Kuhn, T. S, 86

MacIntyre, A. and Flew, A. G. N.,
  12, 32, 83
Marx, K., 64
Maslow, A., 57
Mollegen, A. T., 43

Phillips, D. Z., 76
Piaget, J., 14
Putnam, H., 2

Rudner, R., 24

Shakespeare, W., 112
Stenson, S., 112
Suppe, F., 2, 7, 8, 9

Tillich, P., 30, 41–42, 54, 62, 69,
  82–84, 91ff
Torrance, T. F., 45, 49–52, 56,
  65–68, 71–73, 78, 81, 85–86

Wheelwright, P., 77

SUBJECT INDEX